LOVING THE GAME WHEN THE GAME DOESN'T LOVE YOU BACK

LOVING THE GAME WHEN THE GAME DOESN'T LOVE YOU BACK

BRANDON SWEENEY

© Copyright 2014- Brandon Sweeney
All rights reserved.

ISBN 978-0-9891367-4-7 (paperback)
ISBN 978-0-9891367-5-4 (ebook)

Published by Next Level Press, a division of Complxx, Inc.
www.nextlevelpress.net

For worldwide distribution. Printed in the United States of America
All rights reserved. This book is protected by the copyright laws of the United States of America. No part of this publication may be reproduced, stored in a retrieval system, or transmitted in any form or by any means- electronic, mechanical, photocopy, recording, or any other- except for brief quotations in printed reviews, without the prior permission of the publisher.

Unless otherwise identified, Scripture quotations are taken from the King James Version of the Holy Bible.

All emphasis in the Scripture quotations is the author's.

Contents

Dedication	i
Acknowledgements	iii
Forewords	vii
Introduction	xiii
Chapter 1: It's Your Choice	3
Chapter 2: My First Love	5
Chapter 3: Rejected by My Father, Accepted by Football	15
Chapter 4: I Hate Losing	25
Chapter 5: Putting All My Eggs Into One Basket: What A Risk!	39
Chapter 6: Proving My Love to This Game	55
Chapter 7: Time For A Change	67
Chapter 8: An Encounter with God that Changed My Life	75
Chapter 9: Sports Does Not Last Forever, But I Wish It Did!	83

Chapter 10: The Pain of a Broken Heart	93
Chapter 11: Finding Courage to Let Go	99
Chapter 12: Four Reasons Atheletes Find It Difficult to Let Their Sport Go	105
Chapter 13: Life Without Sports	115
Chapter 14: The Difficulty of Transition	119
Chapter 15: What You Don't Know *CAN* HURT You!	125
Chapter 16: Athletes Have a Purpose Beyond Playing Sports	135
Chapter 17: A Word to Parents and Coaches: What A Difference You Make!	149
Appendix: Real-Life Atheletes' Stories	159
References	171

Dedication

All those ex-athletes whose dreams of going pro didn't come true: you guys are still important, and you still have a purpose in life that is waiting to be discovered and pursued. Just remember, life is not over -- God keeps allowing you to see another day. Know that sports don't define you, but God does.

I also dedicate this book to those athletes who haven't yet gone through what the ex-athletes went through. I want to encourage you to learn from their mistakes and start preparing to live purposefully beyond sports.

Acknowledgements

I want to thank my Heavenly Father and my Lord and Savior Jesus Christ. I am because Jesus is. Without Him, there is no me. My life is seriously boring without Jesus Christ. Before Him, I just existed, but with Him, I am living. Thanks for loving me unconditionally. Your grace has been sufficient in my life, and Your strength has been made perfect in my weakness. Thanks for giving me this seed (idea) in the form of a book. May it bless every soul that reads it, and may You get all the glory.

To my wife, Ashantae Sweeney: Thank you for your support, encouragement, and love. You have really come alongside me to do life, and I appreciate you so much. God has truly given me one of His choicest daughters, and I am excited that we are going to spend the rest of our lives together. You add so much depth to me, and I am thankful for you; God knows I am!!! I love you so much and forever.

I want to thank my mother, Yteria Sweeney, the woman who gave up everything to raise me. She has taught me what it means to sacrifice. She saw something great in me that caused her to lay down what she was pursuing so that I could have a chance to succeed in life. I thank you so much, MOM. You are the strongest woman I know and the biggest giver I've seen. May God bless you through me; and for all that you gave up or lost, may it come back to you a hundredfold.

To Apostle Otis Lockett Sr. and First Lady Sister Lockett: Pastor -- the man who told me, "Go home and seek the face of God to discover what your purpose is, and when you come back from having surgery, let's move forward and never look back." I can honestly say that I have been moving forward, and I haven't looked back. Thank you both for all the support, encouragement, and labor. God has used both of you to unlock my purpose, destiny, and potential. Thanks for caring for me while I was under your leadership. I am better today because you both have been in my life. God bless you and your family.

To my dad, Gregory Norwood: I thank God that after all these years; He was able to bring us together. Ever since you came back into my life, I have felt a sense of completion and peace that has allowed me to move forward. God is redeeming the time that was lost, and I thank Him for every minute of it.

I want to thank my brother and sisters, Clyde, Yliria, and Anna. God definitely knew what type of siblings to give me because you guys played a huge part in my life growing up. God has used you guys to help me grow and to teach me what it means to share and love when you don't feel like it. We have been through a lot together, and I'm glad we are still standing. No matter what it looks like, we are going to make it because I have a promise from God. So don't lose hope. Be strong and courageous.

Acknowledgements

To James Murray: Thanks for all your help and support. You didn't have to stay with me this long to make sure the book was finished, but you did, and I appreciate you. May God send you more customers and prosper you in every way.

To Bryson G. Baylor & Next Level Press: Thanks for coming alongside of me to help me revise this book to make it what it ought to be.

To all the coaches who played a role in my life: Robert Proctor, David Patterson, Dave and Nick Calcutta, George Ragsdale, Alonzo Lee, Chennis Berry, Chris Camp, Jeremy Maxa, and Mark Black. You guys taught me a lot about what it means to be a man in some aspect. I thank God for using you guys to mold me and shape me into the person I am today

Forewords

Heartbreak is common to those who dare to love earnestly without restraint. The remedies to these heartbreaks are even more common. Special songs are written to soothe the pain of the muscle that is buried deep within the chess cavity. Poems and spoken word emerge with an array of hope for the love sick. The hopeless romantic would use the "Blues" to drown out the sorrows caused by a missing love. It has not been quantified the effectiveness of these remedies, however, the literary work that is captured here by Brandon Sweeney can not only diagnose the athlete who loses their identity in the game that they love, but rehabilitate them to achieve a higher calling through practical principles.

Brandon was a remarkable running back with the all the gifts of the trade. He had the balance, strong core, quickness, speed, good hands, hard nose blocker, vision, a high football IQ, and a Walter Payton work ethic that would come out when fighting, clawing and scratching for the last yard, inch or blade of grass. After igniting the crowd with a thrilling run, he respected the game enough to properly thank his teammates for their contribution. To watch him play with such enthusiasm was like meeting a couple for the first time and getting a strong sense that they were meant to be together for the long haul. However, what many may describe as a tragedy in his life, he describes as the inevitable.

Truth of the matter is every high school, collegiate, and professional ballplayer of any sport will experience the separation from their great love called the "Game". I was never more devastated than when I thought I had followed the prescription for success to pursue the highest level in my chosen sport…football. After winning a state championship in high school, then a conference championship in college while leading in all the passing categories but one in school's history, I thought my relationship with the game was a solid one when I received a free agent contract with the Dallas Cowboys (America's Team and I was an American!). After giving it all I had and doing all I knew to do, one summer breeze morning the game was gone from me. Not just for a moment, but forever in the manner that I had known it. Sure I prepared for this day by ensuring that I got my undergraduate degree with plans to pursue a master's degree in education. I was trained to say all the right things in public, like "I'm just thankful for an opportunity to be a part of the game" or "Now it is time to move on to the next chapter or season in my life." All those things sound great but when your identity has been defined in the game, your first introduction to self-worth, confidence, your future plans, your reason for existing is wrapped in something that you can no longer have or pursue.

This is why the transition for athletes to function in mainstream society can be strenuous because of the stronghold that the game has on you. I had to do a deep search down inside to find something to help me transition from the "game" to life. Even though I had been to church all my life, I spent more time with football than I did God. I didn't realize that my purpose beyond the game was far greater than my playing in the game.

It took me several years to figure out on my own how to transfer the valuable lessons I learned in sports to help me survive in life. "Loving The Game When The Game Doesn't Love You Back" is a great work for athletes young and old to gain a powerful prospective into who they are, why they are here, and what it would really matter.

Thanks Brandon for helping us make sense of knowing what to do when the game moves on.

–**Alan Hooker,** *Hall of Famer, North Carolina A&T State University and Mid-Eastern Athletic Conference –*

Can you remember the time when you were growing up in the neighborhood and you emulated or imagined yourself being one or more of the super athletes you had the pleasure of watching on television, or even seeing in person? In my youth, in the 60's and 70's we would attempt to copy and emulate the athletic skills of Bill Russell, Bart Starr, Hank Aaron, Wilma Rudolph, Billie Jean King, Althea Gibson and the list goes on. In today's generation maybe they are emulating and copying the moves and athletic prowess of LeBron James, Walter Payton, Albert Pujols, Serena Williams, Maria Danica Patrick, Sheryl Swoops and the list continues to go on and on generation after generations' to come.

When one looks back and observes what these men and women have done and are now doing with their lives outside of athletics. How many had or even have a plan B? They all had plan A's, which was to be one of the best to ever participate in their particular sport, and they all excelled in that area. This book "Loving The Game When The Game Doesn't Love You Back "is a must read for every person young and old.

This book should be read by every person that has been afforded the opportunity to make a positive difference and a positive influence in the lives' of others, be it in the field of competitive sports or most importantly in person's everyday livelihood.

Brandon examines and proves the importance of having a plan A but most importantly a plan B, through his life experiences he had the opportunity to deal with thus far in his life. Feast on the pages of this book as Brandon escorts you through some of the most vibrant, tumultuous and gratifying times in his life. This book will truly bless you as you journey through the decision every; (young and old), athlete is faced with today and that is learning how to become the best athlete, or learn how to be the best athlete and person that they can be. We as coaches and persons' of influence must teach these athletes how to acquire the ability to formulate a plan A and a plan B for them to have in place, after the roars and cheering of the people in the stands has diminished to a mere whisper.

Isaiah 58: 10 - 12

10: If you spend yourselves in behalf of the hungry
and satisfy the needs of the oppressed,
then your light will rise in the darkness,
and your night will become like the noonday.
11 The Lord will guide you always;
he will satisfy your needs in a sun-scorched land
and will strengthen your frame.
You will be like a well-watered garden,
like a spring whose waters never fail.
12 Your people will rebuild the ancient ruins

and will raise up the age-old foundations;
you will be called Repairer of Broken Walls,
Restorer of Streets with Dwellings.

These passages' of scripture characterize as well as exemplify the person Jehovah- Jireh, Nissi, Shalom, Tsid-Kenu, Shammah, Sabaoth, Raah, Raphah has and continue to anoint and allow you to become as he continue to mold you into for His glory. I thank Jesus Christ for having the pleasure of knowing you Brandon Sweeney and may the Lord of Host continue to bless you in everything you do.

–**David Patterson.** *Former Running Back Coach at North Carolina A&T State University*–

Introduction

First, let me thank you for picking up this book. This is not a typical book about sports but a love story between a man and the girl he almost married called "Football". As you read it and it blesses you, please pass this on to others. I want to get the word out to as many athletes as possible to tell them that they are "more than athletes". At the end of this book, you will also have a chance to read other athletes' stories about what happened to them when their sports careers ended.

Over my years of playing football, I have seen different men whose lives have been greatly impacted by the game, as well as by other sports, regardless of their age, where they are from, or where they are in their lives. I have met both former high school and college players and active players with a love story about their sport. The ex-high school and college players mentioned how they were All-Stars in high school, All-Americans in college, or on their way to the pros. But then an injury, setback, not getting drafted, or being cut from a team ended their careers. They explained the regrets they had about not having a "Plan B" after sports, how empty they felt, how they lacked passion, or how they were just like everybody else — "average." I would ask them, "Who are you apart from sports? What else are you passionate about? What other gifts and talents do you have?"

With frustration on their faces, they were silent because deep down inside, they didn't know. Their stories didn't matter. What mattered was that they felt unfulfilled, they felt like a failure, or they were searching for meaning in their lives. Whether they were "the man" back in high school, an All-American in college, or even had their shot in the pros, they all talked as though life was over. The sad part about their stories is that they felt that their situation could not change—that there was no hope without football in their lives—because honestly speaking, they didn't feel significant.

The high school and college players who are still playing are so sure they are going pro. They talk about how they don't want to end up average or become just another great athlete who didn't make it. Many people have already told them that they can make it if they stay out of trouble and work hard. They talk about how "big-time" colleges are looking at them or how pro scouts are checking them out. They also mention that if they keep their grades up, stay focused, and work hard, then everything will work out just fine because after all, it's not about what you know but who you know.

I wish it was that easy. I learned that you can get straight A's in school but flunk in life. In their eyes, they think they are wise, but in reality, they are deceived because they don't see the big picture. What is the big picture? The big picture is that there is more life after sports.

As I listen to them, I realize that they are setting themselves up to fail. I ask questions such as, "What is your Plan B if your Plan A doesn't work? What will you do if you experience an injury that ends your career? What other gifts do you have? What else are you passionate about? Who are you outside of sports?" With a confused yet falsely confident look, they reply, "I don't need a Plan B because I'm going to the pros; I'm shooting for my dream."

Then others might say, "I'm going to major in such and such or I'm going to get a job if I don't make it to the pros." But when they are honest they confess and say they don't know, they haven't thought about it, or they don't really care. When I talk to these athletes I can't help but see myself. My heart goes out to them because I had the same story, and I too didn't think about life beyond sports.

WHAT ARE YOUR CHANCES?

There are statistics that the NCAA has posted to give athletes a chance to see the possibility of becoming professional athletes. This is not to discourage athletes, but it is to show them that even if you do become a professional athlete, you will still need to be prepared for sports to end.

The table below was taken from the NCAA's website

	Men's Basketball	Football	Men's Baseball	Men's Ice Hockey	Men's Soccer
High School Student Athletes	545,844	1,108,441	471,025	36,912	398,351
NCAA Student Athlete	17,500	67,887	31,264	3,944	22,576
NCAA Student Athletes Drafted	48	255	806	11	49
Percent NCAA to Professional	1.2% 1 out of 75 will go Pro	1.7% 1 out of 50 will go Pro	11.6%	1.3%	1.0%
Percent High School to Professional	0.03% 3 out of 10,000 will go Pro	0.08% 8 out of 10,000 will go Pro	0.60%	0.10%	0.04%

Estimated Probability of Competing in Athletics Beyond the High School Interscholastic Level:

http://www.ncaa.org/wps/wcm/connect/public/ncaa/pdfs/2011/2011+probability+of+going+pro

There are also statistics provided by the NFL Players Association that say that out of 100,000 high school seniors who play football every year, only 215 will ever make an NFL roster — that's 0.2 percent. Of the 9,000 players who make it to the college level, only 310 are invited to the NFL scouting combine — the pool from which NFL teams make their draft picks.

BREAKING THE CYCLE AMONG ATHLETES

There is a cycle that must be broken; it is a cycle that has repeated itself in football and in other sports in our generation and is being repeated now in our younger generations. This cycle is especially prevalent among African American boys who only think they will be successful if they have a ball in their hands. Some feel that sports are their only hope or way out of the projects.

To most athletes, they are defined by their sport. When their sport ends, they lose their identity. It seems as if they lose their motivation to be successful or passion to be great. Some walk around as if life is over, as if they have nothing else to look forward to. Some of their parents never suggested other options when they were young. All they knew growing up was "playing sports is life".

When it's all said and done, when fans stop cheering, and when that player is no longer recognized for his accomplishments, he ends up feeling forgotten, unidentified, and purposeless.

I MADE IT, AND YOU CAN TOO!

My life is a testimony about how I lost the only thing I ever loved — but how I was able to overcome with the help and love of Jesus

Christ. I was able to discover my identity and my purpose. I found new strength, passion, hope, and vision. I thought my life was over, but it was just beginning.

I wrote this book for the many young athletes out there who had a dream to play professionally but fell short of obtaining that dream or for those whose career in the pros ended early. I am here to encourage the athlete who doesn't know who he/she is without sports. I want to encourage all those athletes who think life is over because they can't play their sport any longer. I want to help the athlete whose dream has been shattered and who doesn't know how to deal with the loss.

You don't have to walk around clueless about what to do with the rest of your life. You can live again, and you can be successful. No matter what you go through in life, no matter how bad things are, you can always recover and make a comeback. God does have a plan for your life, but you must believe that a new beginning is possible. If I can make it, you can make it too because I'm no different than you.

1st Stage

Pee-Wee League / Middle School ... Where Sports Capture the Heart of a Child and the Dream is Birthed!

Until a person can say deeply and honestly, "I am what I am today because of the choices I made yesterday," that person cannot say, "I choose otherwise."
-**Stephen R. Covey**-

"To live is to choose. But to choose well, you must know who you are and what you stand for, where you want to go and why you want to get there."
-**Kofi Annan** *Ghanaian diplomat*-

CHAPTER 1

It's Your Choice

I wish someone would have told me as a boy growing up that life is full of choices and that the motives behind those choices were important. I probably would have re-examined why I chose to play football. My perspective on the game probably would have been altered. I would have thought long and hard about what I wanted to do with the rest of my life. I now have an opportunity through mentoring, training, and coaching to meet young athletes who love to play sports, and the first question I ask is, "Why are you playing sports?" or "What made you choose sports over everything else?"

The most common response that I hear is the following: "This is the only thing I am good at doing, and my friends or brother encouraged me to play."

Then I ask, "What do you want to be in life?"

They reply, "I want to be a professional athlete."

They have already decided what they will do for the rest of their lives. The sad part about this type of thinking is that they don't understand that the game will end one day and they may never go pro.

At this stage, the child's heart has been captured by sports. This usually happens when they get their first taste of playing little league or recreational sports. They learn about teamwork, commitment, hard work, and discipline. This is where children choose a particular sport and call it their first love.

Also at this stage, the dream of being a professional athlete is birthed within a child. For some children, this is the only thing they may see themselves doing for the rest of their lives. If this dream doesn't become a reality, they may feel like they have failed.

CHAPTER 2

My First Love

"How did I end up where I am today?"

I remember asking that question when I was 24 years old. My life was falling to pieces. Nothing made sense anymore, and nothing mattered. I thought my life was done. I had nothing else to live for and nothing left to give. I found myself existing but not living. That's how life is when you haven't found purpose.

After a while, I came to my senses and started asking questions. I couldn't accept the fact that I had nothing else to live for. Existing day by day, working a job, and trying to survive didn't sit well in my heart. I started to examine myself, taking a mental recap of my life, and I found myself asking that question: "How did I end up where I am today? Did I make a good choice when I decided to play football?"

The only way for me to answer that question was to go back to where it all started.

I was born on October 14, 1983 in Akron, Ohio. I grew up in the Spring Hill projects with my brother, Clyde, and two sisters, Yliria and Anna. The most amazing woman alive, Yteria Sweeney, raised me. I did not have to choose my mom. God chose her for me. She was an excellent choice because she was the only woman who could raise a boy like me. She sacrificed her entire life so that I could live, meaning she died to herself (dreams, goals, desires, and ambitions) and did what she had to do to raise her four kids. She is my Superwoman, and I thank God for her.

Like many boys living in the projects, I grew up without a father. It didn't affect me at the time because it was a norm in the projects. I didn't believe I needed a father, so I lived my life accordingly. I was rebellious, didn't listen to anyone, and thought I could do whatever I wanted because my father was not present.

Growing up in the projects was fun because we were occupied every day with some type of activity. We built club houses, chased girls, played football and basketball, raced against each other in the street to see who was the fastest, climbed trees, and fought each other. If you grew up in the projects, you knew something was going on all the time. However, though the projects were fun, I never wanted to stay there.

Our family barely made ends meet. My mother worked two to three jobs just to provide for us. People in the projects never saw a way out; it was as if they accepted the fact that there was nothing greater beyond the projects. I believed that though we didn't have enough money and couldn't afford the nice things in life, the one thing I did have that didn't cost me anything was my dreams. I wanted to be somebody important, so I would dream. I wanted to do something with my life because I was tired of my mom having to work two or three jobs to take care of us. My dream was to do something big so I could take care of my family.

I had a desire to provide for my family, but I didn't know how. Even though I wasn't in a position to provide, I still wanted to help. I didn't know what I was good at or what I wanted to do. I didn't want to sell drugs for a living because I had seen too many people get beaten up or killed over five dollars. Going to jail was a scary thought, and I knew my mother would have left me there to think about what I had done!

I decided to dream big because nothing small ever sat well with me. I was looking for an idea that would take us out of the projects. The dream came in the form of a football. It became my ticket out of the "hood" to a better life. This is how I fell in love with football and how football changed my life.

When I first laid eyes on a football, it was love at first sight. Football caught my attention one day when I was walking around outside in the Spring Hill projects. I saw a group of boys playing sandlot football and having fun, but at the same time, it was competitive and nobody wanted to lose. They were playing like it was a championship game. However, I was caught up by the beauty of the game. There was just something about it that intrigued me.

I wanted to play, but I wasn't sure I knew how to play. Other kids were bigger and older than me, and they were playing tackle football without any equipment. I didn't think I would hold up because I was small and frail, as my mother would tell me. My fear overpowered my desire to play, but I kept thinking of ways to find out more about playing until I learned that my brother played with those boys from time to time. I saw him outside playing and having a ball. At first, I was a little shy, so it made me a little distant. I didn't want to interfere in what they were doing.

Sometimes, I thought about introducing myself to the game, hoping we would meet again, but I felt apprehensive about it, so I kept my mouth closed. I tried to put the game out of my mind and go on with life because hooking up with the game seemed hopeless. Besides, I didn't think I had the courage.

One day, I was outside playing with one of my friends. My brother ran over to me and asked me to come and play with him and the boys.

"No. Can't you see I am busy?" I said, trying to act like I had something important going on.

He was persistent and insisted that I come. I thought he was playing around, so I didn't believe him. "What do they want with a guy like me?" I thought to myself. Eventually, I gave in because I started to become curious about why they wanted me to play with them; I left my friend and went to see what all the commotion was about. As we began walking toward the field, I saw how intimidating they looked.

I said to myself, "There is no way they want me to play with them." But I decided to go on anyway.

We continued walking toward them, and I kept thinking to myself, "What am I going to do? I've never played football before. I don't want to embarrass myself around my brother and his friends."

I asked my brother, "What should I do when I get around them?"

He said, "Just be you. Don't worry about trying to impress anybody."

As we were drawing near, I saw that everybody was huddled up around each other I became nervous and anxious, and my hands started to sweat profusely because I didn't know what to expect.

When we finally arrived the guys were waiting on me, my heart started beating a thousand miles per hour, and I felt my adrenaline rushing through my veins. I was hooked all over again.

My brother looked over at me and said, "Yo, Brandon, I want to introduce you to the guys and this great game called football, which is one of the greatest sports around."

Everything about football drew me in: the excitement, the camaraderie, and the passion that people had for it. My brother told me I would be on his team so that he could look after me. I didn't mind that; in fact, I felt safe because I knew he would protect me. At the same time, he told me, "Don't be afraid or let the other guys intimidate you." I thought that was easier said than done. However, we huddled up, and my brother told the guys to give the football to me because I was fast.

I stood shaking in my shoes and wanted to say "ARE YOU CRAZY?," but I sucked it up because obviously my brother believed that I had what it took or else he wouldn't have allowed me to play with him and his friends.

We broke the huddle and jogged to the line where the ball was. The quarterback looked behind him while he called out the cadence and winked his eye at me as if he had confidence in me as well. I stood in the back all by myself, lonely, nervous, and scared out of my mind. While the other guys on defense started talking about how they were going to hit me really hard and make me fumble the ball and quit, I decided to tune them out and focus instead on what I was going to do.

I began telling myself, "You can do this, you can do this." Then all of a sudden, all I heard was "Hike, hike", and the next thing I knew, the ball was being pitched back to me. My eyes were big, and my hands were raised to catch the ball. Once I received it, I heard my brother and his friend's say, "Run, Brandon, run. Follow my block."

I took off running, "juking", and shaking the other guys so they would not hit me. I followed my blockers, used my speed, and found myself in the end zone. My brother and his friends were excited and cheered me on. From that day, everybody knew I had something special and that I would go far if I stayed with this game.

I was confident on that day and felt courageous because I overcame my fear and realized that I did have what it took to play this game. It felt so natural, and the timing couldn't have been more perfect. There was an instant connection, and I felt like I was born to play this game. I felt like football was my soul mate. We connected on every level. I didn't think I would ever find anything else that would make me feel that way.

That day, I knew I would be with football forever. I purposed in my heart to take care of the game, be faithful to it, and give everything I had for it. I knew my life wouldn't be the same.

'NO' DOESN'T MEAN NEVER, JUST NOT NOW

I went home and told Momma about football, but like most moms, she was skeptical about me focusing on anything she thought was a waste of time. I told my mom how much in love I was and how committed I was to the game.

Momma just said, "Yeah, okay. That's nice, but you are too young to be in love. You are only eight years old. What do you know about love?"

I knew she was just being a mom, so I did not pay her any attention. I started asking my brother questions about football like, "What do I have to do to become better at playing the game?" He told me what he could but admitted that he didn't know much about football because he and his friends just did what they saw NFL players do on TV. I understood that I couldn't become a great athlete if I didn't know anything about the game. After playing sandlot football with my brother and his friends, I started to become bored because I felt like I wasn't getting anywhere.

One day, my brother and I started wondering if organized football existed. We didn't have the Internet back then, so there was no way of finding out what was out there. Instead, we used our imagination to picture what it would be like if there was an organization that had football teams for younger athletes. We thought of names for the teams and what it would be like to play for them.

After dreaming with my brother, I went away "sprung" just thinking about the game and how amazing it was. I stayed up half the night thinking about my future playing football. I was determined to put my all into spending time with football. I was in love with the game — maybe just puppy love, but whatever it was, it had my attention.

I woke up the next day determined to find out everything I could about football. I started asking other guys that hung around the game. I tried to spend time playing more sandlot football, thinking that I would learn something. It didn't work because I had nobody to teach me.

I wanted to learn and be taught about this great game. If I had nobody to teach me, then I couldn't fulfill my dream of making it to the NFL. I wasn't satisfied with just playing sandlot football. I wanted more out of football, but I didn't know how to get it.

One day, I saw one of my friends walking home. I stopped him because he was wearing some type of equipment and he looked funny in it. I knew he used to hang around my brother when they played football. I asked him what he was wearing and where he was coming from. He told me it was football equipment and that he was coming from football practice.

Immediately, my eyes lit up, and I took a deep breath and said, "Football practice! What football practice? Who has football practice, and where can I find out more about this?"

He started laughing but began to explain to me about the team he was playing for and the other teams that he was playing against.

I said, "Wow, are you serious? My brother and I were just imagining this, but we didn't know if it existed or not." "Can you tell me where to sign up and how much it costs?" I asked. "The only way you can sign up is by going down to your local library where sign-ups are held. It is called Pee-Wee football," he told me. "The coaches there can teach you everything you want to know."

He went on to say that there was a football team down the street called "South Rangers". They had pretty good coaches, but he warned me to be careful not to waste their time because they coached and taught a lot of kids how to play football. I asked him about the organization and what it all entailed. He explained to me that the coaches make boys better athletes and provide them with skills needed to be effective against other teams on the football field.

My eyes were filled with hope. I immediately ran home to ask my mom if I could hang around the "South Rangers". I told her I could find out about football and learn how to be a better athlete. She gave me one of those crazy looks, as if I had lost my mind, but I was very serious. She told me "no." I was disappointed; she didn't know how important this was for me. I asked again and told her that the coach mentored a team of boys and maybe he could coach me. She gave me a harsh "NO!" to let me know that she was serious. I left it alone after that because I knew when my mom stood firmly about something, she meant it.

I went outside to spend time with my football and to clear my mind. My mom didn't understand, but I knew that being around football comforted me and made me feel at peace. I didn't have a care in the world; as long as football was in my life, I was fine.

I went back inside and before going to bed, I told my football about the plans and the dreams I had for our life together. It silently agreed, as if it was thinking the same thing. The next morning, I shook the dust off my shoulders from my mom's "NO!" and bounced back with a new plan. I waited until she was in a good mood. It had to be soon because football sign-ups were around the corner. I had to get there before it was too late.

I finally caught my mom in a good mood, and I took a risk to ask her again. She still said "no." This time, she told me not to bother her again. My brother saw how passionate I was about football and stepped in to beg my mom to let us sign up. He knew how much I wanted to learn about football. Besides, he wanted to play, too. I felt that my mom wanted to give in, but she thought about how much she would have to pay for both of us, and she stood her ground.

"Aren't you too little for football anyway?" she asked. "And are you any good at playing football?"

She had heard how football had broken guys' hearts once they pursued the game. She didn't want me to get hurt. I told her that I wasn't like all the other guys. I knew my heart was big, and I tried to assure her that football wouldn't hurt me, but after all that, she still did not let us sign up.

We missed the entire season, which made me very upset. I vowed after that to not lose sight of football and to remain committed, even though it was tough not knowing about the game. My brother and I played football 24/7 — rain, sleet, and snow — because that was the only thing that kept us in contact with the game. I watched the games on TV, but it didn't excite me as much as playing. I was determined to play for a Pee-Wee team because I knew this was the first step toward making my dreams come true, and I wasn't about to let anybody stop me.

CHAPTER 3

Rejected by My Father, Accepted by Football

The year was 1990, and from my perspective, it was going by slowly because I couldn't play football. During this time, I remember one day in particular that had an impact on my life. My mother came and picked me up from school to go to court. I rode along, thinking nothing about it because I was just happy I got out of school early. To my surprise, my babysitter- who kept us while Momma was at work — came along with us.

This made me wonder what was going on, so I asked my mom, "Why are we going to court?" I became curious why she needed to pick me up from school.

She didn't say a word. That's when I knew something was up. When we arrived, I sat outside the courtroom with my babysitter because they didn't allow children in the courtroom. I was still clueless about what was going on. After waiting for hours, my mom finally came out. She was furious. I stood there gazing into her eyes and saw pain, anger, and rage.

She kept saying, "I don't know why he doesn't want Brandon. This is his son. He is going to pay for this."

I sat there thinking to myself, "Who doesn't want me? And whose son am I?"

Nothing clicked, but I became angry because I hadn't done anything to anybody; plus, whoever this person was had upset my mom. We left the building, and while we were outside, my mom was still yelling and fussing about whatever happened in the courtroom. As we got into the car, my mom really let go and just broke down crying. The cry didn't sound like she was angry this time; the cry sounded like she was sad for me. I tried to comfort her, but at eight years old, I didn't know what to do.

Then my mother began to shout, "That's okay! Brandon is going to be successful, and he's going to wish he was in his life!"

I was still trying to figure out who she was talking about, so I asked, "Mom, who are you talking about? Who doesn't want me?"

She looked at me and realized that I really didn't know who she was talking about. She began to explain everything about my father. That's when it hit me. I didn't know I had a father. Well, I knew I had a father; I just didn't know he existed because he wasn't a part of my life.

That day, I experienced rejection — what it felt like to be abandoned and not accepted. I wasn't so much sad as I was curious as to why he didn't want me. Never did I think it would affect me like it did. I was so used to living without a father that I didn't think I needed one.

I began asking my mom questions about him. "What is he like?

Do I look like him? Did he play sports?" They were just questions any kid would ask if he never knew his dad. I remember her telling me all she could. One of her comments that stood out was, "It doesn't matter, Brandon, because you are going to be somebody great and successful one day. Your dad is going to try to come back into your life, but it will be too late."

When she said that, I thought about football and how I knew I had to make it to the NFL. Then I would be able to help my mom out. She wouldn't have to work two jobs anymore. I also thought that maybe if I succeeded without my father, he would try to come back into my life and realize the mistake he had made. I became angry, bitter, and hurt, but I knew that I had football, and I felt like it could fill that place in my heart that my father didn't. That was a day that I never forgot because it left a hole in my heart.

After that episode, the spring and summer went by fast as I still kept my dream of playing football alive. We were heading into the fall — time to go back to school. I was still hoping my brother and I could persuade our mom to let us play football. Finally, she gave in one day and decided to let us sign up. We were all at the babysitter' house when she came to pick us up, and suddenly, she asked my brother and me if we still wanted to sign up to play football. I stood up like a rocket shot out of a cannon. I said, "Yes! We've been waiting for you to say that since last year!"

She had been talking to our aunt Connie, who had two boys (T.J., who became one of the greatest running backs (in my eyes) in college football, breaking every record at Wooster College, as well as records in NCCA football; and Tyrell Sutton, Mr. OHIO, who broke the rushing record for most career yards in Ohio, went to Northwestern, and played for The Green Bay Packers, The Carolina Panthers, and The Seattle Seahawks). My aunt Connie told my mom that she had signed T.J. up. She said that he was "the man" on his team and that the team had some great coaches. When my mother asked what team he played for, it just so happened to be the South Rangers. Then, my aunt Connie suggested that my mom sign us up too.

My mother decided to go ahead and invest in us. I didn't think she believed it would benefit us, but she did it anyway. I was happy because I realized that she had accepted the fact that I was going to pursue football, regardless of anyone or anything that was trying to stop me.

We headed down to where the team practiced. The cost was $40.00 per person: a total of $80.00 for my brother and me. We knew Momma was making a sacrifice, so we thanked her that whole day because it meant so much to us. While my mom was paying, I was looking around at the boys who were signing up. I thought, "There sure are a lot of boys coming to sign up."

I became nervous because they all looked better than me, as if they had played before, but I didn't let that get to me because in my mind, even if they had played before, I wasn't going to let them outwork me.

After we signed up, they grouped us together by age and weight. At first, I didn't know why they split us up into age groups, but I went with the flow. Later, I found out that each group taught you different things about football. Each group that you were placed in built on the foundation laid by the previous group.

I told the coach, "I only wanted information about football because a friend of mine told me you could teach me some things."

He looked at me and laughed. I felt insulted and asked, "What are you laughing at?"

He said, "Because everybody here wants to know about football."

I said, "Well, that must be a mistake because they don't love the game like me. And I know that there are a lot of players, but I have plans of making it to the NFL, and playing Pee-Wee football is the first step."

He replied, "Well, get in line and join the crowd because you are not the only one who feels that way." He went on to say that if I wanted to go anywhere playing football, then I had to start at this level.

I joined the rest of the guys but kept the mentality that I was going to come out on top. The coach told me he would teach me all I needed to know about being a football player so I could make an impression on the game. He told me that I had to be willing to listen, do what the other guys hated to do, and do things differently to stand out among everybody else. Then, I would know more about football than other guys and become a student of the game.

The first day he began to coach us was unsuccessful because the training and teaching was hard. The more I thought I knew football, the more I realized that I didn't know anything. I didn't even know what position to try out for. Half of the guys on the team laughed at me because I didn't know what I was doing. I would mess up in drills and lose in competition drills. I didn't know any fundamentals about football, which frustrated me. I just couldn't do anything right, and I felt so embarrassed.

Other guys seemed like they had been doing this all their lives and had more in common with football than I did. They even talked like they knew more about the game than I did, and that irritated me. I knew they didn't have what I had. They even tried to show off to impress the coaches during training — just doing anything to get their attention.

I found out later that they had been there before, so they already knew what to expect and how to act. I was the new guy. It was intimidating being around other guys and not knowing anything, but I held on to what the coach told me and began to work hard day in and day out. I also found out that I was a pretty good running back, but the coach made me a quarterback because T.J., my cousin, was playing running back. He was good at what he did, so I didn't mind; I was just happy to get a chance to play. Besides, both positions touched the football a lot; that I liked.

Sometimes, when practice was over, I saw how some of the other guys' fathers stayed with them and worked on their skills so that they could become better football players. Then, I also saw other guys like me who had no fathers to help make them better football players. That bothered me, and I felt sorry for the other guys, as well. The coach was the closest thing we had to a father figure in our lives. He was all we had as an example; he was the one teaching and training us.

I often asked him how I could become a better football player. I wanted to stand out. He told me that football liked men who were in shape physically and mentally, who paid attention to every detail about the game, who went the extra mile when nobody was looking, who were content but not complacent, who were determined, who would not give up no matter what came their way — men that played with passion.

He went on to say that football liked men who put it all on the line, sacrificing their bodies, their time, and their energy every day. Football loved hard-working men who showed passion and promise, committed men that would give up anything to have this game.

While listening, I started to give up already, because it was such a huge demand and there was such a high price to pay. But then again, my Momma didn't raise a quitter. She taught me to go after what I loved with all my heart, so I stayed the course and took what he said to heart. I had a lot to work on because I was far from football's standard of the type of player it wanted, but I wanted to reach that standard. I knew that I had to compete because the other players were bringing their "A" game every day. I had to be the best; I wanted to be the best because I didn't want to see my mother's money going to waste or me wasting my time. I knew in my heart that I couldn't afford to lose. I had to go all out. I had to prove to myself, my family, and everybody else that I was serious.

For those next few weeks, I did what I had to do to be the best. I would come early to practice because sometimes I didn't have a ride. I would carry my equipment and walk about 8-10 miles to practice. I set my mind to win in every drill or competition. No matter what, I was not going to lose.

I often asked the coaches how I was doing because I was looking for affirmation and approval. They told me that I was improving but that I had a long way to go. I knew if I kept being consistent, then I would do just fine. They later told me about the games we would have to play in order to show what we learned about football and test our athletic ability. They also told me that if I was looking for approval, then I would have to perform well for the crowd during the games.

I knew this would be a great opportunity to shine, as well as gain the approval of the crowd. This was also a chance for me to make a good impression on my coaches. I had no doubt I would play because the coaches knew I had been working hard, but I didn't want to let them down either. I talked to the other guys to see how they felt about impressing the coaches and playing against other football teams. One of them said it didn't matter, as long as he stood out and impressed the crowd. Other guys pretty much said the same thing while others just wanted to win and make their families proud. They didn't seem to have the same concerns as I did, which I thought was strange, but then again, they had been playing since they were seven years old.

Our head coach prepared us by giving a pep talk the day before the game. He told us that since we were on the same side, we had to act like one unit if we wanted to win football games. He gave us a game strategy and broke down the other team. There were some egos on the team that didn't even listen to what he said; it was as if they had heard the speech before and thought it wasn't important. However, I listened to our coach because I knew he had played the game before, and he knew what it took to win. I knew we had to stick together to win, but it wasn't going to be easy.

On the day of the game, the stadium was jam-packed. Not only did the "crowd" come, but all of our families also showed up to watch us play. I became a little nervous because it was my first time showing off in front of my family. If I messed up, I knew I would let everybody down.

I remember standing on the sideline, waiting to get in the game.

My coach had decided to start another guy at quarterback but told me I would get my chance to play. So I waited patiently until he called me into the game. Our team had been doing great, we were winning the game, and my coach wanted me to get my first taste of Pee-Wee football. I ran into the game, and all I could hear was my mom cheering for me on the sideline, and boy, I felt important when she cheered for me.

The coach called "quarterback sweep left". This play was directly for me because he wanted to see what I could do with the ball. Immediately, I became nervous because I didn't think he would let me run the ball on my first play in the game. Nevertheless, I went back to that day when I first started playing this game, when I was in that little, oval-shaped yard with my brother and his friends. I remembered how well I did that day and what I had been practicing. I began to encourage myself and remembered how hard I had been working and what my coach taught me. Now was not the time to back down.

We were in the huddle; I called the play: "Quarterback sweep left on one. Ready, break!" We jogged up to the line of scrimmage; just across that line, the other team was waiting to take my head off. I tuned them out and called the cadence. "Rangers down, set hut!" I turned to my right to fake the hand off to my cousin T.J. and immediately turned my head around to the left. All of a sudden, I took off down the sideline for a 65-yard touchdown! I had outrun their entire team and scored my first touchdown of the season.

That day, I put on a show, and my performance shocked everybody. My teammates loved me, and the crowd accepted me. I knew that I would be a great fit for football. My mom even saw how good football and I were together and agreed that I should continue to play the game because we were made for each other. My mother was so happy that when I was running to score a touchdown, she ran with me all the way down the sideline screaming, "Run, baby, run! You better run, boy! Score! Score! Score!" People thought she was crazy, but she was my biggest fan and cheerleader.

That day confirmed that I knew I was going to be great and make it to the NFL. I went on through other games that year, proving myself worthy of football's love by being consistent and reliable. The crowd loved me, and every time we had a game, they came to see our team play and to watch me grow into the athlete they knew I was destined to be.

I felt good about myself and had the support of everybody, but I wanted to meet an NFL coach. I know it sounds crazy for me to have wanted to meet an NFL coach because I was so far off from fulfilling that dream, but I didn't care. I was dreaming big, so I kept the expectation that one day an NFL coach would come see me play. I believed that it would happen if I stayed focused on it.

Some people in the crowd told me not to worry just because many had strived and failed to make it to the NFL. They told me that I should continue to work harder, improve every day, and believe that one day I will get my chance. I took those words to heart and cherished them because that was the fuel I would need down the road when things started to get rough for me.

CHAPTER 4

I Hate Losing

I went through three South Ranger teams before my mom decided that I had to go to another organization. In each group, I remained consistent from the day I started, and I turned all the coaches' heads, impressing them with my determination, heart, and excellent work ethic. They could tell that I loved football by the way I sacrificed for it. The coaches were good mentors, and they prepared me well to be the best athlete I could be — not only that, but we were always winning games. We probably lost a total of three games in all of my three years with the South Rangers.

Unfortunately, my mom thought I should transfer to another team because we switched neighborhoods; this upset me because I had become close to the coaches I already had. They taught me a lot about the game and how to become a good football player. They were sad to see me go, but they told me to remember what they taught me and to take care of football and it would take care of me.

Over those years, I grew stronger, and my commitment to football also became stronger. I spent the entire summer working out and developing my football skills. Around the neighborhood, people knew me as the star athlete, and I wore that title proudly. I would play football anywhere, in any type of weather, and on any surface. I was that addicted to the game.

My brother was probably even more serious than I was because he had worked a job all summer long to buy a weight set. We were lifting weights at 10 and 13 years old because we wanted to become stronger. My brother would push me every day until I was tired. I didn't like it; in fact, some days I told him I wasn't going to do anything because I thought he was crazy. I still wanted to be a kid and have fun, but looking back, I understand that he wanted me to be the greatest, and he definitely knew what it took. He doesn't know it, but I looked up to him because he had a work ethic like no other.

I had other players that I looked up to, as well; they were some of the most talented athletes I had ever seen. Although they weren't the best role models, they were heroes in my eyes. I kind of understood their situation. We all lived in the projects, and for some athletes, the only way to survive was to sell drugs. Looking back on my childhood, there were a lot of young athletes that were in the drug game because someone introduced them to it. In the long run, it ruined their careers and their lives.

Summertime came, and it was time for sign-ups. My mom apparently had been doing some research, and she came across a guy by the name of Coach Bagley. He was coaching the West Griffins, and he had heard that my mom had taken me off the South Rangers team and was looking for another team to put me on. I don't know what he said to my mom, but that season, I ended up at the West Griffins. I really didn't want to go because they were not good; but when I got there, I found out that they had pretty good coaches, so it wasn't so bad. I was excited, but sad at the same time, because the guys weren't the same.

The guys on this team didn't put forth the kind of effort that showed that they wanted to play this great game. What amazed me was that they had incredible talent at every position but could not win a game. The reason that they could not win was everybody wanted to be the superstar instead of a teammate. I didn't let that discourage me, though. I remained focused and did everything my last coach had taught me. My previous coaches had developed an attitude in me that winning was everything, so I brought that same attitude to the West Griffins.

EITHER YOU LEARN FROM LOSING IN ORDER TO WIN OR LEARN NOTHING AND KEEP ON LOSING!

The coaches decided to put me at running back because I was fast. I guess they figured I could do more damage by playing running back than by playing quarterback. It made no difference to me, as long as I touched the football to show off my athletic ability. It was July, and we were getting ready for the season by coming together to practice. I was still doubtful that playing for this team would do me any good, but I went to practice anyway because my mom wanted me to. When I arrived to practice, I was surprised because I noticed we had a lot of talent on the team. I thought this wouldn't be bad after all, until we started practicing. We couldn't get anything right, everybody wanted to do their own thing, and the coaches didn't seem to have any control over the team. I immediately became frustrated and thought we were in for a long season.

Our first game rolled around, and I was feeling pretty good. I thought it wouldn't be that bad if we just used our athletic ability. Boy, was I wrong! We lost. In fact, we didn't just lose — we were blown out. The other team demolished us, and I thought, "This is it. I am done with this team." After the game, I was crying because I was upset that we had lost. People were looking at me like I was crazy, but I took winning very seriously. I knew if we weren't winning games, then it could ruin my chances of being a great player, so I threw a fit and made a scene with my negative behavior. This went on game after game after game until one day, my running back coach picked me up to go to practice. He had a little talk with me, which at the time I didn't want to hear, but it was very valuable for me in the long run. He said, "Sweeney, you're a leader. In fact, you are a great leader, and the kids look up to you." He went on to say, "But your actions are affecting the entire team. I know you don't want to lose, and I know that you are used to winning, coming from the South Rangers. That is why we wanted you to come play for us. We thought you could help us win, but it turns out that you are adding to our problem." He said, "If you start encouraging these guys instead of yelling, helping them instead of fussing at them when they mess up, then they will respect you and will want to play for you and with you." I sat in the car, silent and shocked at what I just heard. I could not fight or disagree with what he was telling me, but at the same time, I only cared about winning. I thought I would try it, but only so it could benefit me. I am sure that he did not mean for me to take it the way that I did, but that was how I took it and how I was going to use it.

Halfway through the season, I started trying to encourage the players, in an attempt to get them to rally around me or at least have the same passion I had about winning. Nevertheless, it didn't work; we continued to lose games, and I went back to my old self. This time, it was worse: I not only started crying and throwing temper tantrums, but I started saying, "I quit, I quit. They suck — we're never going to win." My mom used to come along side of me to comfort me because she knew I didn't like losing, and she probably thought it was her fault that she brought me to this team.

Something rose up in her one day after a game. I guess she was tired of hearing me complain, so she grabbed me by my jersey and said, "Look at me! Wipe your eyes and stop crying. I don't ever want to hear you say 'I quit'. We don't quit. We never quit!" That day, she must have knocked some sense into me because from then on, the idea of quitting never came out of my mouth. Even when I wanted to quit, I didn't entertain the thought.

We probably only won one or two games that entire season, and every time we lost, I did the same thing. I was still crying, upset, and angry, but I stuck it out the entire season. At the end of that season, I took what my running back coach told me, coupled that with what my mom told me, and I went out recruiting. I was determined that we were going to be better than we were last year. I went to school, and I started noticing guys that had talent and thought they would be great assets to the team. By the time the next season rolled around, we were ready with the new additions to the team.

I took all those losses last year and decided to learn from them. I looked at the man in the mirror and knew in order to win this year, I had to change the way I did things. One of the things I did was take the pressure off myself to do everything. I needed everyone to do their part, and I had to trust that they would. Additionally, instead of fussing and yelling, I became more encouraging. I wanted my teammates to know that I believed in them and that they had what it took to help us win. With those changes, I saw a tremendous difference in our team. We came together as a team and won every game we played, except for one which we tied. Not only that, but we ended up going to the playoffs and ultimately winning the championship.

WINNING FELT GOOD UNTIL THE SPOTLIGHT WAS TAKEN FROM ME

I was thrilled, both because our team was playing well and because I saw myself grow from a little boy to a young man who was taking responsibility for leading his team. However, I discovered that I was, on the inside, still selfish and ambitious, as some of the spotlight was taken off of me. Even though we played as a team and won the city championship, people had stopped noticing me. They began to look at some of our other players, like my best friend Jeffery Swain, who ended up scoring the game-winning touchdown for us in the championship. I was happy for them on the outside, but on the inside, I was jealous and afraid that the momentum and attention I had gained was fading.

I became angry again and frustrated because that wasn't my plan. I wanted to win while everybody praised and cheered for me. I didn't expect for people to give more attention to our other players. It seemed like trying to help other people wasn't working; my dream of going pro was being threatened by me trying to be a team player. At the end of the season, I said to myself that from here on out, it's all about Sweeney.

THE WORST COACH I EVER HAD

I worked my butt off in the summer of 1997, preparing to build my reputation back up in the eyes of the coaches and people. I knew that my last year of playing Pee-Wee football was coming up, and we would get new coaches. I was going from Junior Varsity to Varsity because of my age. Most of the guys from our championship team came up to Varsity, and I knew we had a shot at winning the championship again because we were loaded.

I had no doubt in my mind that I would be the starting running back because I knew there was no one better than me. We had a guy by the name of Thomas Hill who transferred from the East Dragons to our team because his uncle wanted to win. We had beaten his team in the championship last year. We thought he would be a great asset to the team because he could flat-out run. He was one of the fastest guys I saw play football, and I knew with his speed, my quickness, and Jeffery's power, we would dominate the league.

Our coach was a hard coach; he showed a lot of favoritism, and he was all about winning no matter what. I didn't mind all that, as long as he favored me; besides, he was picking me up for practice every day because he stayed around the corner from me. So I knew things would work out in my favor. Unfortunately, he was the type of coach who liked big, fast, strong running backs and thought I was too small to play. He tried to move me to slot or wing running back so that I could use my quickness on the outside. He said that Thomas and Jeffery were bigger than me and would do well running up the middle. He then went on to say that because I was small, I couldn't take the pounding on a Varsity level. Immediately, I was crushed because no coach had ever talked to me like that, let alone tell me that I was too small. I didn't know how to handle what he said. I wanted to cuss him out and tell him about himself, but I knew he was the type of coach who would kick you off the team, so I didn't say a word. My face, however, showed it all.

I went home that day depressed, scared, and nervous because my position was being taken without me even getting a shot. I told my mom what happened, thinking she would take my side, but she didn't. She told me that this was an opportunity to prove myself and to "show them what I got". She told me not to let people tell me what I can or cannot do because if I did, I would only be living up to their opinions, which didn't matter much in the first place. She went on to say, "Don't let no one outwork you; do your best every day." And of course, she let me know loud and clear that I wasn't quitting, no matter what.

I felt encouraged that night, and I decided that I was going to outwork everybody on my team, including Thomas, who took my position. I was on a mission to prove to my coach that I had what it took to play running back at this level, but of course, he didn't notice me. He didn't notice my hard work and the effort I had put in; the only name he would yell was "T Hill". Boy, did that fire me up; I became discouraged because I had never been in this situation before. I was used to getting the coaches' attention, but this time, I was being ignored. I didn't know what to do but to stay the course because of what my Momma told me.

Game day came around, and I was ready. A few coaches had told me they had noticed how hard I had been working and to keep it up. That cheered me up, and I felt encouraged knowing that someone was watching. Then I thought, if they noticed it, then the head coach had to have noticed it as well. There we were in our first game, and like always, I knew people had come to see me do what I did best: run the ball hard and score touchdowns. However, my coach stuck with his game plan and gave Thomas and Jeff the ball the entire game, leaving me with only three carries.

I was pissed off the entire game, which affected my performance. I couldn't believe he would do this to me. I took it personally and felt like he was trying to make me pay for something. I let my attitude show and went the rest of the game playing like I didn't care, but we still won, thanks to Thomas and Jeff.

After the game, I didn't say a word while everybody was jumping and shouting because we won. The truth is, I didn't care; I was still stuck on how many carries I had, with no touchdowns. My mom, brother, and sister tried to congratulate me for the win, but I dismissed it because I didn't want to hear it. My attitude became worse and worse as the season went on, yet we kept winning.

I started thinking about my dream of going pro, taking care of my mom, and making my dad regret not being in my life when I became famous. There it all was, staring right in front of me, and it seemed to fade as my excitement for the game was fading, as well. I tried to rehearse what my mom had said, but it wasn't working. This coach had gotten the best of me, to the point where I didn't want to play football anymore. It was tough coming to practice while I was being ignored, and on top of that, my coach kept comparing me to Thomas and Jeff. He said, "If you were more like them, then I would give you the ball." My self-esteem was being damaged every time he said something negative to me. Every time I did something that wasn't like Thomas and Jeff, he would ride me and tell me that I wasn't good enough. He thought this would make me a man and motivate me to work harder, but that didn't work for me. I wasn't the type of player that got anything out of being yelled at or put down. I knew I worked best when I was encouraged.

I had never been in this position before, where the spotlight wasn't on me. I had never had a coach tear me down the way he did. Game after game, all the coaches and fans wanted were Thomas and Jeff. Day after day, I continued to come to practice and work hard, hoping something would change. I never got my chance to be the star, to be the MVP on the team, because I was overshadowed by my teammates.

I know what people might say: "You are selfish" and "It's not about you."

"At least you are winning." I didn't care about winning if I wasn't the man. That's what I was used to; that's how people recognized me. Nevertheless, I toughed it out until the season was over. We went to the playoffs, but we lost in the first round, and the sad news was that my coach blamed it all on me. He said that if I wasn't being so selfish and played for the team instead, then we would have won the game. I agree with part of what he said, about being selfish, but I also felt like if he would have used me more, then we wouldn't have lost. At that point, I didn't even care because I was ready for the season to end.

After the season, I did a lot of reflecting and self-examination. I decided to not let what my coach said or did to me stop me from reaching my dream. I chose to take everything from that season and use it as motivation. I reminded myself why I started playing this game. I took the goals and dreams that I had written down and rehearsed them over and over again: I was going to the NFL, I would take care of my mom, and no one would stop me.

Brandon during his Pee-Wee football years.

2nd Stage

High School: Where the Relationship with Sports Becomes Serious

I never met a successful man that didn't have a Back Up Plan.

-**Brandon Sweeney**-

CHAPTER 5

Putting All My Eggs Into One Basket: What a Risk!

I attended Firestone High School on the west side of Akron. I really didn't want to go there, but my mother made me because they were known for their academics, not for football. She didn't care if they weren't strong in football; all she was concerned about was a good education. I had no choice but to go to Firestone, since she put food in my belly and clothes on my back. I dared not bite the hand that fed me.

My first choice was Buchtel High School because my family had attended that school, and I didn't want to break the tradition. Colleges knew Buchtel for its winning records and great football players. Buchtel always had great athletes, so I knew I wouldn't have a problem getting a football scholarship.

My mother didn't want me to be concerned with just playing football. She knew that I needed a Plan B, but I was too young and dumb to even think about that. My focus was on going to the NFL. I had already found a basket worth putting all my eggs into.

My first day of tryouts was interesting because everybody on the team talked about college scouts like they knew them well. I heard them say, "You have to get recruited by them if you want to get to the NFL. If you don't perform well, then you are rejected." I heard them tell stories of other guys who went before them and didn't make it to the pros. They seemed confident, as if they knew exactly what to do to get recruited.

I thought to myself, "Why would college scouts come to a school that doesn't win football games?"

The conversations made me uneasy because I didn't want to be one of the guys who got rejected. I was rejected once by my father, so I wasn't about to let rejection happen to me again. I knew I had to do something differently. If I did not, the head coach wouldn't notice me, and I would end up average, like all the other guys that went before me. I sure didn't want to go through what I endured on my last team.

I saw some guys give up without a fight. Others had a chance to get a scholarship, but they allowed women, sex, drugs, alcohol, bad attitudes, poor grades, and parties to distract them. Some had what it took to get there, but they didn't want to work hard. Some guys had the money, but they didn't want to waste it on going to college just to play football. Most guys had girlfriends, and it was hard for them to balance football with a relationship. For many, that became their downfall. Then there were a few who, because they couldn't afford to pay for college, had the will, determination, and heart to do what it took to get a scholarship.

Last but not least, there were guys who just didn't care. When their high school careers were over, they didn't think about going to college. They didn't love football like they said they did, and their actions spoke for themselves. Some were in and out of football constantly because they weren't ready to be serious. I learned that everybody there had a different agenda.

I wanted football for what it offered, and I loved it with all my heart. My actions showed it. I didn't allow anything to distract me. I messed around, but when it came to football, everything else was pushed aside. Most guys just loved the thought of making it to the NFL, but they probably saw that there was too high a price to pay for what they claimed they loved. Football was all I had and everything I needed. If football ever left me, I knew I would be ruined. If nobody else was going to be faithful to the game, I was. The reward of pursuing my dream was greater than the risk of football ever leaving me.

In the beginning of my freshmen year, I was under the radar; I still needed to develop in order to become like the other players who had more experience. I tried to get involved and get under the coaches radar so they would notice me. They kept telling me that I was not ready for the varsity team and that I needed to grow, learn, and patiently wait. I was only 5'7" and weighed 120 lbs. They thought that I didn't have the size nor had mentally prepared enough to play on that level. I didn't see it that way; I was looking at the size of my heart, not my physical size. I knew if they gave me a chance, I could prove them wrong. They weren't like my previous coach; I believe they saw my potential and wanted to prepare me for the next level.

However, I was not complacent when it came to what they were saying. I couldn't stand there and watch the other guys outdo me. I thought college coaches wouldn't notice me if I just sat back and did nothing. I had to have their attention, and I also had to have the approval of the crowd because I drew confidence from being recognized by them. That was a way of life for me, and I didn't see myself doing anything else but playing football. I thought about how far I had come, and I didn't want my relationship with football to end. I started to spend more time practicing every day after regular practices concluded. I began to perfect my skills daily. I got around other players to learn everything I could.

I was hungry for the love of the game and for its acceptance. I had to keep improving and learning. I was not satisfied with what I had learned from my previous coaches.

High school was no joke. One of the coaches often told us that.

"Only the strong survive, and the weak fall by the wayside." I wanted to be the last man standing. I was crazy enough to do what I had to do to prove that I could make it and that I deserved a chance.

Toward the end of my first year, I surpassed my peers. My extra work paid off. At times, I was laughed at or talked about for my extra workouts to improve my skills. Some players were saying that I thought I was better than everybody else. I didn't always feel like I fit in because of what they were saying. Sometimes, I even slacked off working out just so I could fit in with others, all for the sake of being cool.

I woke up soon, though, because I realized that I wasn't made to be average. If people had a problem with me improving myself, then so be it. I had plans, and I had to stick to them.

During my sophomore year at Firestone, my career actually began to take off. Even though I had moved up to Junior Varsity, my coaches decided to play me on Varsity as a backup corner and special teams player. I really didn't want to play any of those positions because I felt like I was weak at them. My favorite position was running back, but I took what I could get because I knew, eventually, my time would come.

I was patient during my sophomore year, and my time finally came. It was during our homecoming game against our rival, the Buchtel Griffins. Two of our running backs had gone down in the second quarter with injuries. My coaches had no other choice but to give me a shot. We weren't having a good season, and we had not been since my freshmen year. I was surprised when they called me into the game, but it was a great opportunity because I was well prepared.

I didn't let the coaches down either. They put me at running back, and I ran as hard as I could. It didn't make a huge difference because we lost the game, but running hard against our rival showed the coaches that I could play on that level at that position. For the rest of that year, I performed well, according to the coaches and the crowds. Just like in Pee-Wee, I had made an impression on the coaches; they loved my work ethic and passion for the game.

I still continued to have the best interest of the crowd at heart. They supported me like they always did, but the attention or recognition I was looking for was from the college scouts. They had more "say so" in whether or not I would advance to the next level. I thanked the coaches for giving me a chance to show what I could do. I let them know how grateful I was for their demonstration of confidence in me.

Making it on Varsity made my relationship with football official, and it got the attention of college scouts, even though our team didn't do that well. We ended that season 2-8, but I gained a lot of experience playing on the Varsity level as a sophomore. That gave me motivation going into the next year.

Coming into my junior year, I was ready. I was running off of my performance from the year before, and I knew that this year would put me over the top. However, we had to face changes along the way; our head coach had resigned for personal reasons. They brought in a new coach named Robert Proctor who had a close relationship with college scouts. His coaching staff (Mark Black, Jeremy Maxa, Chris Camp, Marter, Mike Pechac, among other coaches) made a huge impact on me because they took time to sow into my life. They prepared me for where I was going as best as they could.

The surprise of having a new head coach was both good and bad. I had to prove myself all over again. I had to show that I had what it took. If I showed what I was made of, then I could use that to find favor with him and the college scouts. Everybody had a clean slate, and it was up to the head coach to decide who was committed and who wasn't. This head coach meant business, and I liked that. This was the beginning of a turnaround for our team, which meant no more losing, but winning.

It didn't take long for me to turn their heads. My work ethic and the passion I had for football drove me to be the best. The coach put us through intense training, just to see who would quit and who really wanted to play. He was hard on us, but fair, and he never asked us to do anything that he wouldn't do himself. All he asked was that we do what he said, and he would help us get where we wanted to go. There were times when he asked us to do things that seemed impossible. I thought about giving up, but my goals and dreams wouldn't allow me that luxury. They kept pushing me forward.

In the end, some teammates did quit. Some made it, but some were told that they didn't have what it took to play this game. It was sad, seeing how hard they had worked and how they had pushed themselves to another level to impress the coaches. In the end, they found out that the coaches didn't approve of them and football didn't love them like they thought. I knew that my coach was not playing around when it came to football. His heart was to build character and make us better men. He was determined to weed out the players that didn't want what he was offering.

That day, I purposed in my heart not to take my relationship with football for granted because there were so many of us competing with each other. At any time or any day, I could be dropped like a phone call. I got back to my grind and continued to press forward to accomplish what I had set out to do.

We ended the season 2-8 for the third time since I'd been there, but the games were a lot closer. I did some great things that year, and I excelled among some of the best athletes around. My name became known around the city of Akron, and people were finally taking notice of my athletic ability.

NO ONE IS BIGGER THAN THE TEAM

There was one lesson my coach taught me that I will never forget. During the season, our coach was big on curfews in order to keep us from getting into trouble. Well, my high school was having a dance because we were about to face our rival, the Buchtel Griffins. Our coach told us that we could go to the dance, but we had to leave at a certain time. Whoever didn't leave would be in trouble. We attended the dance but decided to stay a little longer at the party, thinking that our coach would never find out; that was until he sent one of his assistants to make sure all of us had left on time.

To make a long story short, I and a couple other key players were caught. The word got back to our coach, and he suspended us for one game, which was against our rival. When he told us we couldn't play, our hearts dropped because it was the biggest game of the year for us. The two other guys were seniors, but our coach didn't care. He was big on keeping his word and knew that it would benefit us in the end. We accepted the punishment because we disobeyed, but it was painful sitting in the stands watching our team lose 87-6.

To this day, I respect our coach for disciplining us because I knew it wasn't easy for him. It taught me that just because I am a good athlete, that doesn't mean I can do whatever I want to do. There are consequences to everything, and we were no exception to the rules. It also humbled me and made me realize that my actions can affect the other people who are attached to my life. Our team needed us, but we let them down because we were thinking about ourselves. From that point on, I stepped my game up and became more accountable to my team.

DETERMINED TO PROVE PEOPLE WRONG.

I finished the season strong and won numerous awards while competing. I was also recognized as an All-City athlete and MVP. People saw that I was going somewhere. They often encouraged me to stay focused so that I could make it to the NFL one day. I quickly gained the favor of my coaches and others because they saw that I was hungry and that I wanted to be great. My head coach often spoke highly of me to college scouts because in his heart, he knew my passion for football. I also became even more attracted to the game because the fans loved me. Football saw the sacrifices I was making and how faithful I was to the game.

Heading into my senior year, I was becoming an outstanding and well-known man. Big-time colleges were sending me letters every week showing their interest in me. My dream was getting closer and closer, and I knew that "to whom much is given, much is required." I accepted it as a compliment and an honor, but I couldn't let it go to my head. I knew if I did, I would lose sight of my dream and end up like other guys who almost made it but fell short because they allowed things to distract them.

I didn't want to end up falling short of my dream and living in Akron for the rest of my life. I didn't just want to be remembered as a great high school running back. I was determined to make a huge impression on college scouts because it was my last shot. I knew I had to leave everything on the field after every game, until there was nothing left inside of me.

My coaches had faith in me, and they worked with me when the season was over and even during the summer when everybody else was taking it easy. My coach once told me that "while I'm sleeping, somebody else is out working." When I heard that, I was shaken by it because there was no way I wanted somebody to outwork me. My coaches wanted me to be the best. They believed that if anybody should go to the next level, it was me. I was confident and assured that I could not fail because of their help. I learned a lot from them and gained insights about football that other guys didn't know.

I had another outstanding year, with its fair share of hardships and setbacks, but it all worked out for good. We ended the season at 5-5, but our record should have been much better. We lost some close games because of mistakes. This was one of the best teams I had been on during the four years I had been playing. It wasn't because of the record. It was because we had players that wanted to win. The many great things I ended up doing my senior year came because of the players I had around me.

My performance allowed me to gain the respect of college scouts, which made them more interested in me. They even came to see me play against other teams, and they liked what they saw. Besides, my coaches put in a good word for me, which made them even more intrigued.

At the end of my senior season, several college scouts decided that they wanted to give me scholarships to come to their respective schools. I had offers from a variety of schools, ranging from Division 1A and Division 1AA to Division II. They were all impressed by my performance and the highlight tape they had viewed. They saw that I was qualified, and they gave me the green light.

The only problem was that I wanted to play running back, and the schools that offered me scholarships wanted me to play defensive back. They thought I was too small to play running back because I was only 5'8" and 175 lbs. I was very upset because they didn't want me for the love I had for the game and for how good I was at what I did. They didn't want me to play running back simply because I didn't fit their standard. I refused to accept any of their offers because my heart was set on being a running back. I had been determined to prove people wrong ever since my Pee-Wee coach told me I was too little. When I heard people say things like that, I put my guard up and tuned them out.

After a while, the schools withdrew their offers because they didn't want me to play running back — plus my ACT scores weren't high enough. I had a 3.0 grade point average but a 16 on the ACT. All I needed was an 18, but I didn't take it seriously because I was relying on my athletic ability. My coach soon woke me up by telling me how important this test was to getting into school and to securing a scholarship. I then took the test seriously and scored an 18 after five tries. However, the schools still wanted me to play defensive back, and I still refused to accept their offers.

People thought I was crazy for turning these schools down after all of my hard work. They almost made me feel stupid for refusing some of the schools' offers. I didn't care, though, because I still felt that I should fight for what I believed in. I knew I was a great running back, and I knew I could play on that level. I wasn't going to compromise. I knew something better would come and that I wasn't going to pay to go to college.

Months went by, and nobody came knocking on my door. I started to become discouraged. Maybe I should have taken one of those offers because I didn't want to go to a DII or DIII school. No NFL scouts came to those schools unless you broke records and had a good agent, I thought. I continued to wait while my head coach tried to talk some sense into me. I told him, "I'm only going to a school that wants me to play running back and will give me a scholarship."

In April, a coach in Clarion, PA found out that another school had not taken me. He knew my head coach, so they talked and worked some things out. I was heading to Clarion University to play running back on a partial-scholarship.

My dreams were coming true as I stood firmly on what I believed. I thanked my coaches for everything they had done for me. They had gone the extra mile to help me accomplish my goals. If they hadn't helped me, I probably wouldn't have arrived at this point in my life, and I wasn't going to let them down.

I started looking back on my four years of high school. I had built genuine relationships and made more new friends. I had also gained respect both in the school and throughout the community. I was showcasing my talents and growing as a man. I was on my way, as long as I could keep up the good work and keep everybody happy.

My head coach often spoke about not putting all my eggs in one basket – that is to say, not putting all of my hopes and dreams into football. He told me that I needed to live my life and that football would be there if I handled my business. He went on to say that if I took care of football, football would take care of me. I heard what he was saying, but I wasn't focusing on that because football was all I had to live for. In the back of my mind, however, I knew he was right.

I felt that if I stopped paying attention to football, then somebody else would take my place. I was too focused to let go of the game. Football already had my heart, and I was willing to go through anything for the game. I also wanted to help my mom, and this was the only way I could make that happen. I nodded to my coach and left, but before I did, he told me that he was proud of me for making it this far; most men didn't.

v

Brandon during his high school football years

3rd Stage

College...Where Commitment to Sports Is Taken To Another Level

"Unless commitment is made, there are only promises and hopes; but no plans."
-Peter F. Drucker-

"Take the first step in faith. You don't have to see the whole staircase, just take the first step."
-Martin Luther King, Jr.-

CHAPTER 6

Proving My Love to This Game

After graduating from Firestone, I had the entire summer to prepare for training camp in August. Clarion University had great expectations for me coming into football camp, and I knew that I had to be ready to show the coaches what I was capable of.

It was the beginning of August when my mom brought me to training camp. She was a little nervous because she was leaving her baby boy in another state where she couldn't be there for him. She knew I was becoming a man and that she had to let me go. Despite her nervousness, she was proud of me, and I could see it on her face. She knew that I was close to my dream. I was used to her being there at all my games, but I knew that things were changing.

As we got out of the car, we hugged, and I said a quick goodbye because I didn't want it to be long and drawn out. I told her I loved her and that I would see her later. I knew she wanted to hug me a little longer and talk about how she was going to miss me, but I didn't allow her to because it would have made it harder for me.

Leaving Akron was a little tough for me because I missed my old teammates and the relationships I had built, but I couldn't focus on that because I didn't need any distractions. I was prepared to leave behind the familiar in order to pursue the unknown.

FALL CAMP

The head coach at Clarion University was pretty cool. He and my last head coach were pretty close, and they both treated me well.

The culture was different at Clarion, but I settled in nicely. I met players who were really down to earth and very serious about football. I began to develop a new concept of commitment and a new work ethic. I learned quickly that if I wanted to succeed at this level, I couldn't get complacent, thinking that I had it all together. I had to get rid of the ego and the "know it all" mentality. It wasn't like I was the best athlete they had brought in. There were a lot of athletes who were brought in because they were "the man" at their high school, just like I was. I had to learn how to turn the coaches' heads so that they would notice me out of all the other recruits.

The guys on the team were big, strong, and fast, like nothing I had ever seen before. However, I wasn't afraid or intimidated because I had learned not to look at the outward appearance of a man but at his heart; that's where everything was determined. These were grown men, and everybody had to compete for a spot on the team. Excuses weren't allowed.

I was prepared, though, because I took all of my training and applied it. I learned how to improve in my weak areas. At this level, I couldn't slip or mess up. There was no room for error, being new to the program. Besides, they paid for me to come to their school believing that I had what it took to make the team successful, so I had to show them that I was the man for the job, ready to be thrown into the fire at all costs.

DOES IT REALLY MATTER WHAT MAJOR I CHOOSE?

While playing for Clarion, I didn't really take school that seriously because I thought it would interfere with my dream of playing in the NFL. I really didn't take choosing a major seriously either; if I was going to make a lot of money in the pros, what would it matter anyway? I chose Communication because I figured once I was done playing football, I would be on ESPN like most retired athletes. That was about as far as I thought about a career after sports.

I talked to some of the other players on the team, and they guided me on what classes to take and what teachers to get. Playing football took a lot of your time, and you never got a chance to breathe. As an athlete, you just did what you could to get by. It probably wasn't the right thing to do, but it seemed right at the time.

I'M ONLY HERE TO MAKE IT TO THE NFL!

While playing football for Clarion, I had some great times and met some great people. I was fortunate to meet two wonderful coaches named Nick and Dave Calcutta. They saw something special in me and took a liking to me. They decided to teach me new things about football to prepare me for the next step in my career. I was honored because it seemed like there was always somebody in every school I attended who took me under their wing and taught me about football. I didn't take that lightly either because I knew only greatness would come out of it. I would finally be able to show football and everybody else that I meant business.

While there, I worked extra hard, believing that if I turned the heads of the coaches, they would realize that they had made a good investment.

We were given four years at the college level (with an additional year in case we had to sit out for personal reasons) to show what we could do. NFL scouts were active on this level. Everybody tried their best to perform well so that it would be them on the scout's radar. If you impressed the NFL scouts, then you were on your way. I wanted my dream of playing in the NFL to come true because I had been faithful for years, sacrificing, struggling, and fighting to get to where I could finally make a name for myself.

Usually, college coaches allowed players to come in right away to show their athletic ability. At this program, they were looking for the best of the best to be on their team. The training was ten times harder than the training at high school. I went without seeing my family for a long time, and I was often homesick because I didn't know anyone. I felt unimportant, whereas I had felt very important back home.

As players, we gathered around each other and supported one another because we knew it was hard being so young and away from home. We all had one goal: make it to the NFL. We were willing to do whatever it took to get there.

Many of us talked about how it was going to be. I often dreamed about the many great things I would do. The dream was priceless, and it made the process seem short. Nevertheless, I still had to encourage myself when it got tough, and it did get tough at times.

However, my freshman year was incredible. I stood out among the best and came out on top. My coaches were impressed and told me to keep it up. If I continued to perform well, then I would definitely get the NFL scouts' attention. I even amazed myself with my performance. My family supported me, and the fans loved me. I gained more confidence in my ability to play at the college level, and I was encouraged to continue doing a good job.

I shocked a lot of people back home. There were people who were expecting me to fail. They were hoping I wouldn't make it, but I used that as motivation to prove the doubters wrong.

When you are passionate about something, you go after it with all your heart because failing is not an option.

Going into my sophomore year at Clarion, I was being praised by fans and the community. They were looking forward to great things. As always, I worked even harder by doing the things that other men hated to do. Reaching my goal and fulfilling my dream was right around the corner. By the end of my sophomore year, I succeeded in becoming one of the best running backs around, and I was honored with an award for doing so well that year.

I was accustomed to standing out, but this time seemed different. I couldn't put my finger on it. Fans continued to support and encourage me, my family was always proud of me, and my coaches didn't seem to have any complaints. I guess by this time they already knew what I was capable of.

TRUE COACHES, NOT ONLY WANT THEIR PROGRAM TO BE SUCCESSFUL BUT THEIR PLAYERS TOO. SOME COACHES ONLY USE ATHLETES TO MAKE THEIR PROGRAM SUCCESSFUL.

After that year, I developed an attitude that everything was going to be about me. It seemed as if everybody on the team was out for themselves. New running backs were gunning for my position, and I felt that if I decided to help them, they would steal what I had. I was insecure, but I didn't let the other guys know it. Even though we were all really close, I still had to look out for number one because at the end of the day, it was all about me.

Our head coach didn't make it easy because he put us against each other so much. He played favorites, and he would tell me one thing but do another. After a while, I started to figure him out and realized that he didn't care if I made it to the NFL or not. He was just using me to make himself look good. I found out that he had been lying to me about how much he wanted me to make it to the next level. All he cared about was what he could get out of me and how many games he could win. Behind my back, he was doing everything he could to see that I failed. He made promises that I would get a full scholarship, my books would be paid for, and I would get more carries as a running back. He didn't keep any of his promises and for that reason I felt like I had made a huge mistake in coming to Clarion.

I became frustrated with him because I had trusted him and looked up to him as a mentor. I thought he was leading me down the right path. I told him how I felt about football, and I did anything and everything he asked of me in order to gain his approval. What was I to do now? I loved football, but I didn't see how I was going to make it when he was trying to sabotage my dream.

I decided to keep an eye on him, but I also stayed focused on the task at hand. I knew I was there only for a season, and I couldn't get sidetracked.

SOMETIMES YOU HAVE TO LEAVE THE PLACE OF COMFORT IN ORDER FOR YOUR DREAM TO SURVIVE.

My running back coach, Dave Calcutta, heard about the situation and told me he would help me. He said that I was better than Division II football and that there were plenty of schools that could use a good running back like me. He went on to say that if I was interested, then I could transfer out of Clarion. My eyes lit up with joy because he had given me the answer to my problem.

Immediately, I started looking up other schools to see if they would accept me. The process was not easy. When my head coach found out, he tried to do everything he could to keep me, but it didn't work. He also told me that I wasn't good enough to go to another school and that all I would be was a back-up running back that sat the bench.

I started to believe him because, after all, he knew more about football than I did. However, I dismissed the thought; I was willing to leave Clarion so that my dream could live. I didn't know what I was getting into by leaving, but I was willing to find out. Anywhere was better than being there. I wasn't going to allow him to mess up my dream of going to the NFL. More than anything, I just couldn't allow my hard work and dedication to count for nothing, so I persevered until another school would accept me.

While still in pursuit of a new school, I managed to finish the spring semester at Clarion, decided that I wouldn't return, and went back to Akron. My good friends did everything they could to make me stay, but in my heart, I knew I had to go and step out on faith. It was hard leaving behind people I had grown close to, but I had to trust that I was making the right decision.

SOMETIMES ALL YOU NEED IS THE MISSING LINK

On my way back home, after wrapping up the 2004 spring semester, something happened to me that words could not describe. I felt like I was missing something in my life, but I didn't know what it was. With all that was going on, from trying to find a new school to dealing with my coaches, I was exhausted. I needed guidance and direction. I couldn't think or function. I wanted to play in the NFL and become this great running back, but none of it seemed like it was going according to plan.

I felt an emptiness that football could not fill. This empty feeling continued for a month. Then, one day I woke up, and I decided to stop doing things that weren't helping me become a better person – I found that I no longer had an appetite for such thing. I had been having sex, partying, smoking, and drinking because it was the thing to do. In my heart, though, I wanted to change and to start doing right; I just didn't know how.

Then I remembered my friend Isaiah's mother, Ms. Stewart. She used to tell me about Jesus Christ in high school. She used to say that Jesus Christ was going to save my life and I would surrender to Him. I thought she was crazy at the time, but for some reason, that morning she was on my heart. When I got back to Akron, I called her and told her I wanted to go to church. I asked her if she could teach me about Jesus. When I arrived to meet with Ms. Stewart, we went to a Bible Study, and I remember the preacher making an altar call about giving your life to Jesus Christ. I remember having my head down, feeling nervous about going up.

Then I felt a peace in my heart that assured me it was okay to walk up there, and when I did, the emptiness that had been in my heart was filled with the love of Jesus Christ.

This love was indescribable. It was like falling in love all over again, except His love was different: it was unconditional. His Word pierced my heart and cut to the core; God told me through a pastor that He had great things in store for me and my destiny possessed greatness. If I trusted Him, then He would do exceeding abundantly above all that I could ask or think (Ephesians 3:20). I held tightly to that Word like a newborn baby to a bottle of milk.

When I decided to give my life to Jesus Christ, everything felt new, and my life was changed. That entire summer of 2004, I was Ms. Stewart's disciple, and she taught me about Jesus Christ. She taught me how to walk by faith and trust God for everything. She also taught me how to pray and read the Bible to become more acquainted with who Jesus Christ was.

Jesus was the missing link that I needed; I knew He would right every wrong in my life. I also thought that He could really help me to be the great running back I desired to be. With His help, I couldn't fail. I knew that He would take me where I needed to go, if He was who He said He was.

KEEP ASKING, SEEKING, AND KNOCKING. SOON YOU WILL HAVE WHAT YOU HAVE ASKED FOR, FIND WHAT YOU WERE SEEKING AFTER, AND THE DOOR WILL OPEN THAT YOU HAVE BEEN KNOCKING ON

My search to find a new school seemed meaningless at one point, and it left me wanting to give up. I couldn't give up, though, and I kept thinking about football and all of my dreams and plans. In the Word of God, I found where it says in Galatians 6:9 NLT, "Don't get tired of doing what is good. Don't get discouraged and give up, for we will reap a harvest of blessing at the appropriate time."

That encouraged me to keep on searching. Eventually, I found a school in Greensboro, NC, called North Carolina A&T State University. They welcomed me, but the only problem was that I had to pay my own way because they didn't have any scholarships left. They said that if I worked hard, they could possibly give me a scholarship down the road. That meant I would have to be the starting running back.

I took the offer and ran with it, not knowing how I was going to pay my way or how I was going to get there. When I gave my life to Jesus Christ, I stopped trusting myself and started trusting Him. I knew this was too big for me to handle, so I stepped out on faith and believed that my dream was worth the risk. By August 2004, I was at North Carolina A&T State University and more on fire than ever.

Brandon during his tenure with Clarion University

CHAPTER 7
Time for a Change

It was August 2004 when I arrived on A&T's campus, by the grace of God. I began talking to the coaches immediately to see where I would fit in. I only had two years left to play football, and I had to make those years count. The coaches were impressed with the highlight tape I had sent, and my running back coach from Clarion had put in a good word for me. That really made them curious about what I could do and what I was all about.

In the meantime, they decided to red shirt me which allowed me to sit out for a year since I had transferred up to a Division 1AA school. By NCAA rules, I had to sit out a year. I used that red shirt year to my advantage by spending time working on my football skills. Everything was different now, and I had no time to waste. I used my time to prepare because I knew the opportunity to perform would come. I had to have everything in order.

I always seemed to find good men who were down to earth and I ended up developing solid relationships with them. No matter where I went, every athlete I talked to was in love with football or knew about the game. Some of the guys told me their plans and dreams of going to the NFL and making their family proud. They all had the same plan and dream. All I could think of was "What if I didn't make it? What if the NFL scouts didn't approve of me? What was I going to do?"

Reality had finally set in. It was possible that the NFL scouts could find somebody better than me. Other men were just as passionate about football. I got rid of all distractions, and I put all my time and energy into football. I also prayed to God that He would allow me to make it to the NFL. I felt that He would see the desire I had, and I wanted to put my relationship with Him first. I believed that my favor with God would set me apart from the others.

The Bible says in Psalm 37:4 NLT, "If you delight yourself in the Lord, He will give you the desires of your heart." I believed He would do that for me. I was trying to do everything He wanted me to do so that He would give me what I desired.

NOW THAT YOU PUT IN THE HARD WORK, IT'S TIME TO GET PAID. IT'S SHOWTIME

The waiting period was over. I was like a hungry lion trapped in a cage. The coaches gave me an opportunity to show my ability in spring practice and I didn't fail them. They were shocked, and they immediately fell in love with me.

I knew I had to make a good first impression because there were players just as good as me, if not better than me. In the end, it seemed that I was able to capture their attention and hearts. They also decided to pay for me to stay in the program by offering me a scholarship. I didn't have to pay anything out of my own pocket, and this excited me.

I eventually became the starting running back for A&T. In my first debut as an Aggie was in the Aggie-Eagle Classic against North Carolina Central University. I was nervous but full of excitement an adrenaline. I knew it was show time and I wanted to display to the crowd that Brandon Sweeney belonged here.

I will never forget that game because I rushed for 150 yards and scored 3 touchdowns. Though we lost the game, which was disappointing, I had become the man in the eyes of the Aggies. The next day an article was written about me that stated "Aggies lose game but finds a new Running Back in Brandon Sweeney."

I was being recognized for my ability. Plus, the Aggie fans were just too good to me. They were encouraging, and showed their "Aggie Pride" at every game we played in. Without them, I don't know where I would have been because they always gave me hope to keep going forward. Also, my running back coach from Clarion kept in contact with me to cheer me on; he congratulated me on my successes and for being faithful to the game.

I had a great first year though I missed three and half games due to an ankle sprain. That threw me off track from becoming a 1,000 yard rusher since the great Maurice Hicks who played running back for A&T in 2000. I ended the season with 877 yards with 7 touchdowns, and I averaged 107 yards rushing per game. My best game was against Morgan State University. I was coming back from my ankle injury and ended up rushing for over 200 yards with 4 rushing touchdowns. I also scored the touchdown in overtime to seal the game. My future was looking bright and I knew it could only get better. Finally after all the hard work I had put in it was paying off.

I found a place where I could fit in and become content but not complacent; my goals hadn't been accomplished yet, and I never lost sight of that. My performance that year attracted some NFL scouts, and to my surprise, they took an interest in me. That comforted me. I said in my heart, "Finally, my dream is soon to come true."

YOUR SUCCESS SHOULD NOT REPLACE GOD BUT GLORIFY HIM

At the end of my first year at A&T, I had high hopes for what the next year held for me. I had already started making plans to prepare for the upcoming season. I was at peace and felt certain that nothing could get in the way of my dream. I thanked God because He had helped me to get where I was. He had worked everything out for me by opening the door in Greensboro, NC. He had made all of this possible.

I started building my relationship with God more because I wanted to show my gratitude and appreciation for what He was doing in my life. I wanted to know more about Him; but after walking with God for several months, I had hardly spent any time with football. I tried to reason with myself about dedicating more of my time to football so that I could maintain my performance. Suddenly, it seemed as if God was taking the place of football.

When I thought about it, I felt that football would understand. I believed that if I took care of God's business, then He would take care of mine.

In my mind, I continued to struggle with the fact that I was giving all my time to God and not so much to football. Playing football demanded a lot of time, especially when I worked out; I always spent extra time away from team practice to become a better athlete. I thought about my dream of going to the NFL and what it took to get there. I knew if I slacked off going into my senior year, then the scouts would probably back off.

I thought about other men who wanted football as much as I did. I thought about how they would give everything to make it to the NFL. I thought football would understand because I had been faithful and committed all these years. I didn't think it would hurt if I cut back on doing extra work after practice. I was faced with a dilemma, and I didn't know what to do.

I didn't want to lose football, and I definitely didn't want to lose God! My heart was torn between the two. Months went by as I tried to let it blow over. Eventually, I prayed about it because I wanted to get this off my chest.

I told God, "I don't want to lose football, especially after being with the game since childhood. Football is important to me." I guess He heard me, but I didn't get an answer.

At least I was honest — I still wanted Him in my life, but at a distance so that football could still be #1. At the same time, I felt that God was tugging on my heart because He wanted to be #1. He wanted to be first, and He wanted me to spend those extra hours with Him. I struggled with that because I had never seen myself giving anybody more time than I did football; but something in me just couldn't let God go, and I didn't know why.

I loved and trusted football because it had been there in my life when nobody else was there. It was my comfort zone, my safety net. Football had a stronghold on me that was hard to break. I had only known God for less than a year, but His love somehow seemed to outweigh football. For the life of me, I couldn't understand it.

I wanted them both to have first place in my heart, but it was causing chaos, and I wanted peace. In the Bible, I knew God was a God that didn't want idols put before Him, and when I gave my life to Him, He had become Lord over my entire life. I didn't believe that God had a problem with me playing football, as long as I didn't worship the game, but for me, not worshipping the game was hard to do. I then realized that football was an idol in my life. In fact, it was my god because I did whatever it demanded of me. The decision to make God first seemed easy, but I didn't understand how I was going to put football in second place when it had been in first place since day one.

BE CAREFUL WHAT YOU PRAY FOR

January 1, 2006 rolled around, and I remember saying to God, "Lord, I love you, but I also love football. I want to play in the NFL because that has always been my dream, but let me get through my senior year and after that, you can do with me what you want because my life is not my own." I said that prayer with the intentions of surrendering my life to God and to do what he wanted me to. However in the back of my mind I was hoping that I wouldn't have to give up Football in the process.

The Aggies Brandon Sweeney rushed for 151 yards on 32 attempts while scoring three quarter.

Brandon while at NC A&T State University

CHAPTER 8

An Encounter with God that Changed My Life

I started the year off by setting goals and getting everything lined up for the season, but God had other plans that would shake my entire life.

In February, I had an encounter with God that completely changed my life. Our church held a men's retreat where men went off to the mountains to have an encounter with God. I went because I knew I had been wrestling with some decisions I had to make and bad habits that I wanted to get rid of. The retreat lasted from Friday to Sunday and we weren't allowed to have contact from the outside world to remove any distractions. There at the retreat I met God in a powerful way that I had never met Him before. I saw men being delivered from all types of habits, broken hearts were being healed and restored, and men that were prideful become broken and humbled before Jesus Christ. That experience was amazing and unforgettable. As a result of all this, I had a stronger desire to get to know Him more.

EVERY GREAT EXPERIENCE YOU HAVE ON THE MOUNTAINTOP EVENTUALLY LEADS YOU BACK DOWN INTO THE VALLEY

When I got back from the mountains I was filled with the love of God that I wanted to share it with anybody I came in contact with. There was no way I could keep what God was doing in my life a secret. I began to share what God was doing in my life with other men on the football team, and God began to change their lives. I eventually started a bible study called Athletic Christians Taking Sports (A.C.T.S). I wanted to provide a place where athletes could come and share their faith and develop as a person. God was showing up and showing out.

I had a new perspective about playing football. I felt confident and at peace that my senior year would be one of the best years of my career. So, I continued preparing for the upcoming season because I knew I had to do well to impress the NFL scouts.

Going into spring practice we had new coaches that we had to adjust to since our last coaches were let go because we didn't have a winning season. This divided our team because the new coach didn't seem to care for some of the players. However I tried to convince our team that if we came together we could still have a successful year.

Our team was working hard and finally coming together as a unit. We were hungry and determined that we would not have another year like we had the previous year. Everyone was doing their part and most of the players were attending our bible study on Wednesday nights.

On April 1, 2006, our coach wanted to have a team scrimmage to evaluate what type of players we had on our team. During this time,

An Encounter with God that Changed My Life

walk-ons and red shirt freshmen were getting their chance to show the coaches what they could do. I didn't have to compete because the coaches knew what I could do, but I wanted to compete anyway. I didn't want the other guys showing off while I stood by and did nothing

During the scrimmage, my coach asked me to come and run one more play before taking me out of the scrimmage for good. I went back in, and while running with the ball, three defensive players tackled me. Immediately, I went to the sideline with a sharp pain in my side. I tried to shake the pain off, but it was still there. Soon, it became worse, and I fell to the ground. Some of my teammates sent for Rob, our trainer. I will never forget him; he saved my life that day. He ran over to examine my condition. As he approached, the pain intensified. He touched me to locate the pain, but I wouldn't allow him because the pain became worse. At that moment, he knew the situation was serious.

He asked if I could get up and walk to the locker room. I mustered up enough strength to make the attempt, but it was unsuccessful. I tried again but to no avail. I tried a third time, but I still couldn't move, and the pain had grown even worse. That's when I knew that my condition wasn't good. I began to cry because I had never experienced anything like this. My whole football career flashed before my eyes. I asked God to help me — to not allow me to go out like this.

Rob ran to get the cart to take move me from the sideline to the locker room because I couldn't walk. When he arrived, I saw Tim Shropshire, one of my best friends and teammates. I immediately asked him to start praying for me. My other best friend and teammate, Quante' Speight, assisted me and joined Tim in prayer.

As the pain grew worse, it limited my movement. Every time I tried to move, I felt sharp pains rushing through my entire body. I couldn't even take off my football equipment; it took too much strength.

When I got to the locker room, Rob ran to get the van while Tim and Quante` stayed with me, trying to keep me from passing out. When Rob pulled up, they gently placed me in the back of the van and rushed me to Moses Cone Hospital.

When I arrived at the hospital, I did not have to wait long because my condition was serious. By that time, my eyes were rolling in the back of my head, and the doctor had a hard time trying to take my vitals. They rushed me back to a room to examine my condition and found out that I had ruptured my left kidney. The doctor told me that they would perform immediate surgery to drain blood and urine from the kidney that ruptured.

After the surgery, the doctor came in with news I thought I would never hear. He told me that because of the damage that my kidney had suffered, it would have to be removed. He also said that I would never be able to play football again. I only had one good kidney remaining. He explained that playing any contact sport with one kidney could put me at serious risk for more damage. When I heard, "You will not be able to play football anymore," I tuned him out. It was like having a bad dream and waiting to wake up. I thought to myself, "This has to be a joke. He must have the wrong patient. Does he know what he just said? Does he have any idea who I am? He must not know that I'm supposed to play in the NFL!" When I snapped back into reality, I started praying to God, asking Him to heal me.

I thanked the doctor for sharing the news, but in my mind, I rejected everything he said. I didn't see my whole career going down the drain like this. The doctor told me to get some rest and to think about having my kidney removed..

    I had a lot of thinking and praying to do; I knew God was up to something, but I didn't know what. My faith and hopes were high because I was expecting God to perform a miracle.

    I was in the hospital for three days. During that time, some of my friends and teammates and people from my church came to see me. Some of the coaches even showed up to make sure I was okay. I was grateful that so many people had visited. I really felt cared for and loved. I didn't think that many people would show up to check on me. Tim Shropshire, Quante` Speight, Justin Spears, Choey Gilreath, and Tia Hutto all came, along with others who stuck with me for the entire three days. I couldn't have asked for better friends than that. They also encouraged me to be strong, trust God, and to know that everything would work out just fine.

Brandon while at NC A &T State University

4th Stage

Sports…Marriage, ' Til Death Do Us Part!

Someone once said, "You don't marry someone you can live with; you marry someone you cannot live without."

I say: "Play sports because you live; do not live to play sports.
Play sports because it is a part of your life and not life itself."

-Brandon Sweeney-

CHAPTER 9

Sports Does Not Last Forever, But I Wish It Did!

When the doctors finally released me from the hospital after having to drain the blood and urine, they placed me on bed rest for almost a week, but I was frustrated because I was ready to get back to football. Nevertheless, I had to follow the doctor's orders so that I could heal properly.

While on bed rest, I thought about football and all my teammates. I wondered if anybody had missed me or if I was just another athlete with great potential who had failed to do anything with it because of an injury. I thought about how my football career could be over and how my injury could prevent me from ever playing in the NFL. I didn't want to end my career like this. I didn't want to be remembered as the guy who went for the dream but didn't make it.

After the week of bed rest, I was fully energized and ready to get back to football and school because the school year was coming to a close and I had finals coming up that I had not prepared for. I went to school to finish the semester as best I could, and I went to my coaches to explain what the doctors had told me. I told them I needed to have my kidney removed and that the doctor told me I would not be allowed to play football. But it was my choice.

After explaining everything, the office was filled with silence. They had dejected looks on their faces, as if all hope was gone. It seemed like they had already written me off but couldn't find the words to tell me. For them, the most important goal at that point was for me to get my education and not to worry about football.

They didn't realize how much passion I had for the game. I was a fighter, and I wasn't going to quit. Surely they knew I could bounce back from this setback. What they were saying was a hard pill to swallow. I was looking for approval, comfort, and encouragement. I wanted to hear that it was okay and that everything would work out just fine. I wanted them to tell me, "We support you, and we will help you get through this."

I wanted them to say something to kill the empty silence, but by that time, I felt a lump coming up in my throat. I tried to fight the tears from rolling down my face. I turned and walked off, crying uncontrollably. My relationship with football was coming to an end.

I rested like the doctors had told me, but I still felt pain and uneasiness. It wasn't from my kidney; it was from my heart being broken. I prayed and prayed that God would heal me, but He did not answer me. It was as if He had planned the whole thing from the beginning. Though He didn't answer me, I knew He saw what was going on. He had the answer, and I was determined to get it.

I began to encourage myself in God. I purposed in my heart that I was going to stand on the Word of God to heal my kidney. I believed that God wouldn't let me end my career like this and become a failure. The doctor wanted me to have the surgery, but he didn't give me all the reasons why. People kept telling me to have the surgery to be on the safe side. Others told me to hang up my cleats and move on with my life.

Nobody understood my heart. I didn't have a problem with the surgery, but I wasn't going to have it "just to have it" when I knew God was a Healer. It just didn't sit well with me. If God wanted me to have it, then I would have it, but if not, then I would be standing on Him and what He was able to do in my situation.

Everywhere I turned, it seemed that nobody believed that God could heal me. The only person who really stood in agreement with me was one of my best friends, Justin Spears. He told me that if I believed God could heal me, then he was going to believe with me. That encouraged my soul and strengthened my heart because it showed me that somebody supported me.

Summer came, and I was still praying and still believing that God would heal me. I did everything I could to get Him to talk to me, but He wouldn't say a word. Everybody thought I was crazy because I still hadn't gone through with the surgery, but I wasn't going to go through with it until God gave me an answer. I wanted to know if He wanted me to have the surgery or if He was going to heal me. I also needed to know what to do before school started again. Time was going by so fast that I struggled with making a decision.

By the middle of July of 2006, God spoke to my heart and told me to have the surgery. He wanted to get glory out of the situation. I agreed with him because I knew He knew the right answer. I was just curious about why He had waited so long to give me an answer.

I believe He waited because He wanted to get my attention off of football and focused on Him instead. He had me right where He wanted me, and I fell for it all in a good way. I prayed, cried, and read the Bible faithfully all summer so that He would tell me what to do. During those times, I became more acquainted with Him, and my relationship with Him became stronger than what I had with football.

I told my coaches that I had decided to have the surgery. They agreed that it was the best thing right now. I told my friends and family, and they were all happy that I had made that decision. In the back of my mind, I wondered what would happen to me and my relationship with football. Everybody was so happy about me having the surgery that they had forgotten about my love for football. But I hadn't.

I figured that I could have the surgery and still return to football. It would be a great witness for God to display how awesome and powerful He is. I reasoned that this would be the way God could get the glory. Unfortunately, when I processed everything in my mind, I realized that football was leaving me. It was moving on without me.

Football doesn't wait for any man, no matter how good or great that player is. The game keeps moving on.

In my heart, I felt like I was going through a breakup with football. In my own little world, there was a dialogue between the two of us.

This is my best description of that dialogue:

I told football that I was going to have the surgery and that I figured we could put our relationship on hold to give me time. Football whispered to me that it was over between us. Football said it was leaving me because it didn't have the patience to wait for me. Football told me that by having my kidney removed, I would become a liability and not an asset.

Football went on to say, "Besides, I have no room in your heart anymore because God took up too much space."

I refused to believe what I was hearing. I told football, "Don't talk like that because I don't play when it comes to our relationship." Football said that it wasn't playing; in fact, football was serious because it had found somebody who was better than me — somebody who would become an asset instead of a liability. Football gave me my ring (my heart) back and walked out of my life.

When those words fell on my ears, it seemed as if life itself had been sucked out of me. I stood there motionless, stunned by what had just happened. My mind began to rewind back to when I was a child, back to all the fun we had together. I cherished every memory, but my stomach turned in knots just thinking about the smell of football and all that we had been through.

When football left me, my life and identity left with it. My heart was broken. The pain I felt was so excruciating that I couldn't explain it to myself or to anybody else.

After I snapped back into reality, the pain was still there. In my heart and mind, that is how I felt football was responding to me. I didn't know how to handle football leaving my life. I didn't know what could be worse than losing the very thing I loved. We had a lot of history, and trying to move on would be tough. Nevertheless, I had to deal with this problem that was tearing me apart.

THE QUESTION MOST PEOPLE FIND THEMSELVES ASKING IS "WHAT IS MY PURPOSE IN LIFE?"

I met with my pastor, Otis Lockett, Sr. He is one of the greatest men that I have come across in all my years of living. I thank God for him. I talked with him about how I wanted to have the surgery in Greensboro. That didn't sit too well with him. He insisted that I go home because I needed to be taken care of by my mom. I agreed, but I told him I had some issues I had to take care of that were preventing me from leaving. He told me not to worry; he would take care of those issues.

What I remember most about the conversation was that he asked me if I knew my purpose in life. At first, I wanted to give him an intelligent answer; but deep in my heart, I felt like that would have been a front. I told him from the heart that my purpose was playing football and making it to the NFL. Then I told him I also wanted to help people but I didn't know in what way, so I just stuck with my first answer. He looked at me, as caring and loving as a father would be to his son, and said, "I understand that, and that is good, but what if football ends one day? Then what will you do?"

He also went on to say that football is a means to an end and that I needed to think beyond playing football.

He said, "Go home, seek the face of God, and allow Him to reveal your purpose to you." He didn't know it at the time, but that didn't help me because that wasn't what I wanted to hear. He was right, but I just didn't want to hear the truth.

I went back to Akron in July 2006 to have the surgery. While I was there, I decided to take Pastor Lockett's advice and seek God. It was hard because I didn't know who I was anymore.

Nothing seemed to make sense to me; no matter how much I was seeking God or reading the Bible, I just didn't understand myself and why football decided to leave me. My head kept telling me to leave it alone and go on with my life, but my heart wouldn't let me because we had been together for fourteen years. It was hard just throwing all that away. I began to think about all the guys that football had kicked to the curb. I thought about how my fans, coaches, and teammates had been there for me. Where were they now? I had no support, no audience to perform for, no self-confidence, and no hope for my future.

Everybody began to ask me questions about why we broke up and what I was going to do now. I couldn't give them an honest answer, so I told them that we were taking a break and would be back together soon.

I thought about what my pastor had asked me: "What is your purpose?" I had come to a conclusion. I had no purpose, and whatever I did have, I had given to football. My life was invested in the game. What did I have to show for it? Nothing!

As time went on, I came to my senses and tried to figure out what I was going to do. I asked God a million times: what did He want to do with my life? He never gave me an answer or any clues that would lead me or reveal my purpose. I often became frustrated because I couldn't understand why I was in this position. It was like God had me in a wilderness, as if He was trying to break me and test my heart. I didn't know why I was going through all of this but whatever He was doing in me, He sure had my attention.

FINISHING IS BETTER THAN STARTING: GOING BACK TO SCHOOL TO FINISH WHAT I STARTED.

September 2006 came around. It was time for me to have the surgery. Up until that time, I was relaxed and confident that everything would be all right because it was God's will. The surgery was a success. They kept me in the hospital four days. Then I started the healing process after I was released. It didn't last long because God gave me a quick recovery, and I was back on my feet in less than a month.

Life was starting to look good, even though I still didn't know what God wanted me to do. I just enjoyed being with Him. I believed that in His timing, He would reveal the purpose He had for my life. I also felt some assurance when I heard my pastor tell me, "God will never take something away from you without bringing something better back into your life."

I talked to my coaches to let them know I was doing well. I wanted them to know I was coming back to finish what I had started. I also wanted to see if they would still pay for my tuition. They were glad to hear from me and happy that I was doing well. They told me they would pay because they still wanted me to get my degree. That made me so happy and put joy in my heart. I didn't think they would do it since I couldn't play football anymore.

I got off the phone and told my mom the good news. She had been worrying that she would have to pay money, which she didn't have. Mom was a real blessing during my surgery and during those hard times of not being able to play football. She made me feel like a king by taking care of me the way she did. I didn't have to ask or want for anything. I thanked her so much because she didn't have to do it. I LOVE YOU,

MOMMY!

She was also hurt that I was hurt by my predicament with football. She always thought that I would make it to the NFL. The fact that I was so close made her even more upset than I was because she knew how much I loved the game. She comforted me with the love and nurturing care that only a mother could give her son. She, along with God's strength, helped me transition through this process, and that made it much easier to get through.

Not being able to be around the game while I was at home really helped me deal with the pain; as they say, "out of sight, out of mind." As long as I didn't see it, I was fine. I just didn't know how I would react when I did see it again. That time would soon come, as I needed to return to Greensboro for some unfinished business. I pumped myself up into thinking that I could handle it, but I was in for a rude awakening.

COLLEGE FOOTBALL

Top rusher out for season

Brandon Sweeney of N.C. A&T faces kidney surgery

Coach Lee Fobbs (above) must find a replacement for Brandon Sweeney.

Brandon featured in the newspaper about his devastting injury.

CHAPTER 10

The Pain of a Broken Heart

C.S. Lewis said that "God whispers to us in our pleasures, speaks in our conscience, but shouts in our pain."

I believe that is true. God uses adversity and pain to get our attention, even though it hurts to our core. Athletes are taught to endure pain and go through suffering; "what doesn't kill us only makes us stronger," some say. For some of us we have a hard time dealing with loss, especially when we are passionate about something or when we are used to winning all the time. Some athletes have a tough time letting their sports go because, for many, it's been a part of their lives since childhood. It's all they know.

I don't think everybody understand athletes. Some say "Just move on. Leave it alone, and live your life." But that doesn't make sense. It's like a man working for a company for years and suddenly getting fired or laid off. He is confused and lost because, in his mind, he has been faithful to this job. It's hard for him to let go because he has developed an attachment to the job. When people say, "Stop pursuing your sport," "Just give it up," or "You're not cut out for it," they are really saying, "Find something else." But is it that easy for an athlete that is in love with his/her sport?

Not everyone goes pro — only one out of a million. As athletes, that is hard to accept and understand. In part, the statistics are right, but the people who are telling athletes to "get over it" can't understand the pain or frustration because they may not know what it's like to lose something they love dearly. My pastor once said, "If people don't understand your pain, then they will never be able to prescribe you a cure."

I lived in the shadow of my sport all my life because it gave me confidence and support when I thought no one else supported me. The relationships I built in football made me feel like I belonged. When I performed well, fans cheered. Or when all the attention was towards me, it made me feel important. I proved to people that I was good and successful but at the end of the day it all didn't seem to matter.

So I understand the pain that athletes feel when they cannot play the sport they love, and I understand why it is hard to let go. But what if this pain means something? What if this brokenness moves you to something else that is greater than playing sports? What if God can take this pain and brokenness and make something good come out of it?

I believe this is something worth looking at because the truth is, you can dream again! Failure has no name or identity unless you decide to name it or identify it yourself. Who said you were a failure? Did that came out of your own mouth or from what society taught you about failure. You still have your life to live, and you can still do something great with it.

What happened to all the passion, motivation, and drive you had to be great and successful? You lived like nothing could stop you when you were playing sports. You were "the superstar" in your sport. Everybody knew you would be successful one day or do great things, but what happened? Why are you not living? Why have you given up on yourself? There is no excuse in the world for why you cannot still be successful and great.

God has given you a big toolbox filled with gifts, but you decided to take one gift and use it to fix every part of your life; it doesn't work like that. For instance, if you try to use a hammer to fix everything in your house, what do you think will happen? You're going to have a mess, and your house is going to look jacked up.

Let's say that you lost your hammer and everything in your house still needs to be fixed. Now, you feel like you can't work because you don't have your hammer. Do you let everything fall apart in your house? Did you forget that you have a toolbox filled with tools? So it is with your athletic ability — the hammer in your life. You were fixing everything with it, and once you lost it, you allowed your life to fall apart because you thought you couldn't fix anything without it. My pastor used to say, "The devil is a liar!"

Open God's toolbox of gifts that are inside you. Discover those hidden gifts that you haven't used in years. Pick up that gift that you forgot about. Stop making excuses, and get the job done! Stop walking around sad because you lost your sport. Start dreaming and living again, and let the game go.

5th Stage

The Struggle to Let Sports Go

"There can be no deep disappointment where there is not deep love."
-Martin Luther King, Jr.-

"God can heal a broken heart, but He has to have all the pieces. God is closest to those with broken hearts."
-Unknwon Author-

CHAPTER 11

Finding Courage to Let Go

I arrived back in Greensboro in the spring of 2007 with a new mindset and a fresh outlook on life. I didn't want to lie to myself and think that I was over football. I wasn't. Actually, I stayed in shape after my surgery just in case things started to work out. I didn't know if my team still needed me. I was prepared for anything.

I talked with my running back coach, and he was glad to see me. He asked if I was ready to get back to work, and I said yes. He told me they missed me and could have used me the whole time I was gone, but they had done what they could without me.

I was happy to find out that I was not forgotten. I heard that some people were expecting me to come back. They were talking about how the team needed me last year and how I would have made a difference. I was surprised because I thought people were expecting me to hang up my football cleats. My heart started beating fast. My mind began to race back and forth because I couldn't believe what I was hearing. This couldn't be true.

It was hard to believe, but they showed me an article about myself. The article talked about how I had to leave school for surgery and how I stayed strong through it all. The article also explained how I was encouraged and in good spirits about everything that took place. They said it touched a lot of people, and they couldn't wait for me to return.

I didn't know what to do. I had been preparing the whole time for football, but I didn't expect this to take place. I was overwhelmed. The feelings, memories, and love all came back, and I had a desire to play again. I was willing to take the risk because my heart really couldn't take being without the game.

I thought I was content with just being with God, but something about my first love that still had me. When I got around the game again, I knew that I had been fooling myself. I had to make another tough decision if I should pursue playing again or let it go for good. I really needed help!

By the time spring practice rolled around, I had made the decision to get back on the field, but I wasn't sure about my decision. I knew that for now, I wanted to play football, so that's what I did. I kept asking myself what to do, and I prayed as usual to ask God what I should do.

While I was practicing, it seemed as if I had never missed a beat. It was like I had picked up right where I left off. My friends and teammates tried to convince me that I needed to stay on the field because I looked good playing and they definitely needed me.

Hearing those words made me believe that they were right. After all, the game and I had history. I continued to practice with the team to improve. Some people didn't think it was a good idea since I'd had my kidney removed. They were right, but I didn't want to let them know that, so I took it slow. I didn't want to rush anything. We had just broken up, and here I was again, falling for this game, my first love.

People couldn't understand my heart and love for this game. I guess I was willing to look like a fool again for a game that was bound to hurt me again, but I didn't care.

Some of the coaches was excited that I was back but was apprehensive about me playing because I had one kidney. They wanted me to stop playing and finish school. They were more concerned about my health than I was, and they had a good point. They wanted me to stay around the game to help out with the other guys, but how could I be around something I loved that deeply and not participate? If I couldn't play the game, then I didn't want to be around. They saw that I wasn't going to let up or take no for an answer, so they let me play.

AT SOME POINT, YOU NEED TO MAKE A DECISION.

Not long after, I began to feel uneasy. I wasn't sure about my decision. I knew I wanted to play again, but something just didn't feel right. The more I meditated on why I felt like this, the more it seemed like I was making a wrong move. The odd thing was that I prayed and asked God what I should do, and once again, He didn't answer. (I don't know why He does that, but it always seems like He knows that I already know the answer.) It's always hard when it comes down to simply making a decision when so many things are at stake. I also wanted to be sure that I was not just giving up or quitting on football. Staying committed had been ingrained in me as a child, and I never wanted to seem like I was giving up just because things got hard.

I waited to let time sort things out. This wasn't a decision I needed to make right away. In the meantime, fans, friends, and teammates didn't make the decision easier. They kept saying that I shouldn't give up on football because I was great at it. Most of the time, my mind swayed that direction because after all, football was my first.

However, my heart wouldn't commit to that decision. I didn't feel at peace. I asked myself, "If I stopped playing, would the fans and other people still love me? Would they even recognize me without the game?"

I was used to being the center of attention everywhere I went when I played football. Football made me who I was. Without it, I was a "nobody." People couldn't say my name without mentioning football. I kept thinking that it seemed right to keep playing. I didn't have my own identity without the game.

I couldn't let it go. I was afraid to be without football. I was afraid of what people would think or how they would view me if I didn't have football in my life. I felt like I needed football so that I could be somebody. If I didn't have that, then who would want me? My self-confidence, self-worth, and self-esteem all came from football.

At this point, I was frustrated and confused. I didn't know whether I should leave or stay. One day in June 2007, God spoke to my heart in a still small voice and told me, "The only reason you are still hanging onto football is because you don't believe that I have something better for you."

At that moment, the peace of God surpassed all my understanding. I instantly dropped the game, believing that God had something better for me. To this day, I don't miss playing the game, not one bit. I had never thought the day would come when I would let the game go, and to be honest, I don't think I would have let it go if God hadn't spoken to me. However I was glad that I was able to make a decision.

After rejoicing and being happy that I was able to let the game go, I forgot to ask God "What is Something Better?" So I asked Him, but there was no response. This time I didn't become frustrated like I have previously but this time I decided to take Him at his word and believe that He had my best interest at heart. I knew whatever It was it had to be bigger that playing sports. However I wouldn't find this out until I dealt with obstacle that I had been stumbling over since I was a child.

CHAPTER 12

Four Reasons Why Athletes Find it Difficult to Let Their Sports Go

These are four reasons that I have explored with athletes regarding why they find it difficult to let their sports go. These reasons are not meant to discourage athletes from pursing their dreams or to deter them from being around sports for good. Instead, these reasons are for those athletes who are struggling to let go of playing their sports. If they have a desire to stay around sports because they love it, then that is a good thing. However, these 4 Reasons are meant to show athletes who want to POSSIBLY let the game go why the decision is so difficult. These reasons are also for those who are ready to let the game go but don't know how.

Athletes, remember that you cannot play sports forever, and at some point, you will have to LET IT GO. Here are the 4 Reasons why that process is so challenging:

Reason #1: Promises athletes made to themselves or others — these are known as "inner vows".

Have you ever heard the saying, "A man is bound by his own words"? I have experienced this in my own life; I made so many promises and found myself so bound by what I said that it was hard for me to let go of certain things and people. For instance, I remember in high school I was dating this girl, and I used to say that I was going to marry her and that I was going to be with her forever. When I said those things, I meant them wholeheartedly, even when the relationship ended because she wanted to be with someone else, I still couldn't let the relationship go. I tried to let it go, but I couldn't because of the promise I had made to her and myself.

I went through depression and was very discouraged because I was trying to keep her with me when she didn't want to be kept. After I met Jesus Christ, He delivered me, healed me, and gave me the grace to let her go. He then showed me why I couldn't let her go before: I had made an inner vow. What is an inner vow? I like to use Dr. Henry Malone's definition from his book, *Shadow Boxing*. He stated that "inner vow is a vow made early in life. It is made with deep emotions often in a response to a person, experience or desire."

This vow is made to ourselves and is often forgotten about as we get older. When people make inner vows, they are bound by what they have said – especially when they use the words "I will never" or "I will always".

When I found this out, I was totally blown away; I didn't know people could be bound by what they said. I then understood the power of one's words. I connected this idea to the issue of athletes letting go of their sports, and I discovered that the athletes I came across had made promises in their childhood that bound them.

Some athletes, when they were younger, made promises or inner vows to themselves and to others but when sports ended for them, they couldn't figure out what went wrong. For example, some probably said: "I promised my mom, dad, friends, and family I would make it pro even if it killed me"; "I will never give up on chasing my dream of playing professionally"; "I'm not going to end up like these other athletes who didn't make it to the league"; "I have to make it to the league in order to become successful"; "I will never be like my dad. I am going to become famous so he can see that I made it without him"; or "Mom, don't worry. One day, I'm going to buy you a house and get you out of the projects."

Most athletes don't realize that when they make promises they can't keep, it does something on the inside of them, and they naturally feel like it's their fault.

These inner vows tend to bind or keep athletes from maturing and growing. When their dreams of going pro don't become a reality, depression and discouragement set in because they're wondering what went wrong. Could this be why it's so hard for athletes to let sports go?

There is nothing wrong with proclaiming what you desire, but what happens when that desire is not fulfilled or that expectation is not met? There are some athletes who have made inner vows and have seen them come to pass, but this is not the case for everybody.

In order to break inner vows, you have to go back to your childhood and recall the promises you made to yourself. Forgive yourself, let yourself off the hook, and ask God to help you walk in truth. When

I did this, I was free, and I felt a weight and burden lifted off my shoulders – the weight of blaming myself and beating myself up for not keeping a promise that I couldn't keep.

Reason #2: Bond or athletic attachment

Another reason why athletes have a difficult time letting the game go is the bond or athletic attachment they have created. When you spend time, share experiences, create memories, or grow with someone or something, you create a bond or an attachment. That bond can become so strong that if interrupted or disconnected abruptly at any moment in a person's life, it can cause hurt and pain.

For most athletes, these bonds (or what I like to call "athletic attachments") are established between them and their sports. This is developed from over the years of spending time with a sport an athlete loves. The saying goes "You have to drink, eat, and sleep your sport if you want to become successful." That has some truth to it but only if it has a balanced perspective. However, an athletic attachment can become bad when athletes become so dependent on their sports that they lose their identities.

An athletic attachment makes it hard for athletes to let the game go because of the time, effort, and energy put into becoming a superior athlete, creating memories, and sharing experiences.

Nevertheless, this athletic attachment can be broken when an athlete puts sports in their proper place, begins to embrace a new identity or role outside his/her sport, and discovers something else that he/she feels passionate about. This means he/she will have to spend time in a career or hobby that he/she really loves and enjoys in order to let the game go.

Reason #3: Fear

Fear is probably one of the biggest reasons why athletes cannot let their sports go. The unknown makes them afraid. This is normal for individuals who have immersed themselves into something for their whole lives. It's the fear of losing — losing significance, losing support, and losing confidence. When an athlete doesn't know how to replace those things, it can be scary, so most athletes stay put and hang on as long as they can until something happens. When athletes stay in fear, they will not move to action. When they don't know what is next, they will stay put.

First, let me say that being afraid is okay; I definitely understand that feeling, especially when it comes to making a transition. You have a lot of concerns that are legitimate, but you as an athlete cannot stay fearful because it can paralyze you and keep you from embracing your future.

In order to overcome fear, athletes must use two things: faith and courage. First, they will have to embrace faith. Faith is something God has given every human being, and it can empower us to do great things. Faith overrides fear. Faith is a confidence that knows there is something better than playing sports that hasn't been discovered yet. Faith can come by hearing from God. It pays to have a Bible or to be around people who can hear from God. Whenever you hear from God, it brings faith that cause you to act in a way that you couldn't before. Hearing from God brings an assurance that your situation is temporary because He has a plan and purpose for your life.

Another way to overcome fear is to have courage. Nelson Mandela said, "I learned that courage was not the absence of fear, but the triumph over it. The brave man is not he who does not feel afraid, but he who conquers that fear." If you don't conquer your fear of letting go, then you will never know what you could have gotten in return.

Reason #4: They are not ready

Most athletes are simply not ready to let sports go, and that is fine. Some athletes will continue to play until they feel like their time is up or until they reach their goal of winning a championship or receiving an award of some sort. It is discouraging for athletes to have to leave their sport before they reach their goal because of the thought in the back of their minds of what they didn't accomplish.

Most athletes will continue to chase that dream of playing in the NFL, NBA, MLB, etc. because they don't want the feeling of regret that says, "What if I had…?" This is normal, and I commend a lot of athletes for persevering.

The three questions an athlete should ask are the following:
1. When will I be ready to stop playing?
2. Do I have a plan in place for when my sports career end?
3. Who can I find to support me while I make this transition?

These are questions athletes will have to ask themselves while they are chasing their dreams.

4 PRINCIPLES THAT ATHLETES CAN FOLLOW TO UNDERSTAND HOW TO LET THEIR SPORTS GO:

1. You don't have to go through trial and error when you can learn from others. Find someone who has walked away from their sport successfully and learn how they did it.
2. Never stay around something or someone that you are trying to get over. In order to get over your sport, then it's best not to hang around it for a while. Out of sight out of mind.
3. If someone is good at what they do (a professional), then it would be wise for you to listen and let them help you. Seek out professional help that can assist you in making a successful transition.
4. If you try to figure it out by yourself, then you might become discouraged and give up. Find a support system that can encourage you and walk with you while you are going through this process.

6th Stage

Transition from Sports to Life… Where You Find Out How To Function and Live Apart From Playing Sports.

"Readjusting is a painful process, but most of us need it at one time or another."
-Arthur Christopher Benson-

"It is a sad fate to be well-known among many but unknown to yourself."
-Unknown Author-

CHAPTER 13

Life Without Sports

Picture this, if you will—You are just getting over not being able to play the game anymore when someone suddenly comes up to you and says, "I know who you are…you used to…you did this and that…why don't you play anymore? What happened?"

Immediately, your mind goes back to those glory days. You remind yourself of how good you used to be and how everybody knew who you were. Fans cheered for you and supported you. You remind yourself of the preferential treatment you used to get and maybe how many women you slept with (or not but whatever the memory that floats back up).

Then you wake up to reality and realize that those things are gone. All you have left are old highlight tapes, stories, and memories. You are trying to bring back what you used to do so that you can feel that passion and excitement you once felt. You tried being a security guard, working at group homes, and bouncing at nightclubs. Nothing worked, and you found yourself stuck saying, "What's next?"

The problem is that you are still trying to be an athlete even though you are not actually playing anymore. You are having a difficult time transitioning from sports to life. Transitioning from something you have known all your life to something unknown can be frightening. Human nature doesn't like change, especially when leaving something we have given our hearts to. Trying to live without the person or thing that helped you live is like trying to breathe on your own without God's help. It's just hard to do.

If the truth be told nothing fulfills some athletes like playing sports. Deep down inside their heart keeps pulling them back to the game because it is familiar and comfortable. Working a job doesn't feel right especially if they don't love what they are doing, and anything else they attempt to do makes them feel out of place and uncomfortable. This is normal when one is going through transition because the experience is, by definition, NEW.

I have heard so many athletes say that they just can't leave their sport alone or that they don't have anything else to turn to but sports. They hang on and fight tooth and nail, believing and hoping that their sport is going to work for them or that they still have what it takes to play the game. I became frustrated because I wanted to help them, but I couldn't because I didn't have the solution yet; I was still trying to figure it out myself.

Some family members, friends, and fans may have labeled you as just an athlete. They may have put limitations on you and stuck you in the box that says, "Athlete Only." It's a box that limits to what you can or cannot do or become.

Staying inside that box for so long may have caused you to accept the labels and opinions of others. When people see greatness on the inside of you, compliment you, or believe that you can do something else, you have a hard time believing it if it doesn't pertain to playing sports. Sadly, you can't identify with what they are saying because in your mind, you are bound by just being an athlete.

I believe you do want to make the transition, but you don't know how. I believe you want to get on with your life and be what you were destined to be, but you may have no one to help them. I think you got so wrapped up in your sport that you forgot you are a person, too, with problems, issues, concerns, and feelings. If you learn how to navigate through this transition process I believe you will not only survive but thrive in your next endeavor. Life can still be sweet with playing sports.

CHAPTER 14

The Difficulty of Transitioning
(my story continued)

The summer flew by and before I knew it the fall (2007) was here already and school was back in session. I had completely forgotten about the word God had given me. I honestly didn't know how to proceed after it because there were no other instructions so I did the best I could. When school came back so did my struggle with football. I knew I was not going to play ball again but I didn't know how to adjust to life without it.

One day I stopped by my running back coach office to see how he was doing. I was telling him about how I had been feeling and he asked me if I wanted to help coach. He thought I was a positive person and could use my influence to help the other players. He hoped that the passion I had for football would rub off on the other players. The decision was tough because I knew I would be around football every day if I said yes. I didn't know if I was ready. It would be like a drug addict being delivered from drugs and going back to the same environment. I didn't want to relapse, so I gave it some thought.

I actually felt like my coaches genuinely wanted to use me to help make the other players better. I thought about it for a couple of days, and I came to the conclusion that although my time playing football was over, I could help other players go further than I did. I gave in and told my coach that I would help him out.

The season was starting up, and as usual, the guys were getting ready through training. I was ready to help out in any way I could. While going through the training, I was cool, calm, and collected.

Once the season started, we were headed to our first game against Winston Salem State. As we entered into their stadium, I heard the crowd cheering and screaming Aggie Pride. Immediately I had a flashback that took me back to when I first played the game. The beauty of it captured my heart. Every feeling I thought I had gotten rid of came back. I was overwhelmed and filled with conflicting emotions. I became depressed because I wasn't out there on the field. I was excited because the atmosphere made me feel like nothing in the world mattered but this game but I was also bitter because I should have been out there playing in my senior year. I felt discouraged because for the first time, my name wouldn't be heard over the microphone. Perhaps people had forgotten "Brandon Sweeney" and what he did. I realized that I was fooling myself — I really couldn't handle being around the game.

I was trying to keep it together, but I couldn't. I was torn up on the inside, trying to hide the pain that I thought I had gotten rid of. I kept saying to myself, "Dang! Why did this have to happen to me? I was supposed to be playing." I thought to myself, "What went wrong?"

I held myself together as much as I could, but after the game I told my coaches that I couldn't help out anymore because it was too much for me. They understood. They told me that they had been there before and knew that it was hard, and they congratulated me for hanging in there as long as I did.

They encouraged me to finish school, even though they knew that I couldn't play football again. They had allowed me to keep my scholarship which was a tremendous blessing. Normally, something like this doesn't happen to athletes if they are not playing anymore, but they were gracious to me.

IT'S NOT THE END BUT THE BEGINNING

I knew that I had to do something to get my mind off football so I begin a journey to discover who I was outside of this game. It would happen that for the next year and a half, I spent time trying to figure out who I was. I felt like I was going through the stages of a baby all over again, trying to walk, talk, and discover myself. But as time went on I became discouraged, depressed, and eventually it led to suicidal thoughts. I found myself drafting from God, questioning if he loved me, and wondering why He let this happen to me.

When I went to class during the day I kept my happy face on as if nothing was wrong with me but on the inside I was loss and frustrated. When class ended I headed home so I could be alone and during those times at home alone the thought of taking my life crossed my mind. I reasoned in my mind that if I couldn't play ball anymore or find meaning in my life then there was no point in living. I told myself that I was a failure and didn't deserve to live. I told myself that I had blown it and that I would never do anything that matters in life. There I was, holding the knife to my neck and the words "Do it, Do it, nobody will miss you and nobody will care" came into my mind which increased my urge to end my life.

For some reason I managed to put the knife down and I eventually fell asleep. The next day and the weeks after, this struggle would continue. I tried everything I could to stay around people so that I wouldn't have to go home but nothing worked. I tried staying busy but everything I did was boring and purposeless. It was like I was living life with no excitement, no goals, and no dreams. I found myself fighting every day just to live. I worked odd jobs to survive, but in my heart, I longed for hope and for something that would give me a reason for living. I asked myself over and over again, "What's next? Is this it?" I began to cry out to God "There has to be more, God you said there was more, you said there was something better" "Where is it? Where is the better because what I am experiencing is worse? Where are you when I need you?"

Then one day while at home the battle continued but this day was different. While I was contemplating rather or not I would take my life, I heard these words "Brandon I love you and I do have something better for you. This is not the end but the beginning." For the first time in weeks I had felt peace and hope again. I knew that I was not alone but God was actually there with me. The thoughts of suicide fled and I was back in my right mind.

God began sending godly people into my life to encourage me. The times I felt like giving up — the times I felt like what I was going through was too hard to bear — He would send people to lift me up and tell me to keep on going and don't stop fighting.

During those times I was feeling like a "nobody", but God told me I was somebody. I was feeling like a failure, but God told me I was a success in the making. I was feeling like a loser, but God called me a winner. I was feeling like my life was over, but God said it was just beginning. I couldn't quit because I had a purpose and a destiny waiting for me. As I pursued God like never before He begin showing me what was in my heart so that I could see the damage that had been done to it in order to be healed.

CHAPTER 15

What You Don't Know *CAN* Hurt You!

When I look back over the years I played football, I think about all the awards and trophies I received, the championships I won, and the records I broke. I think about how I was loved by people because of my ability to perform on the football field. I remember the many so-called "friends" I had. I remember people liking me because they knew that "Brandon Sweeney" was going to the NFL. I also think about how much attention and recognition I received. I would have thought that those things would have satisfied me, in spite of me not making it to the NFL. I had a pretty good career, but I found that I was still unfulfilled.

There was something in my heart that left me empty, and I didn't know what it was. I believe now that it was an issue that God wanted me to deal with. I didn't know where to begin until God started showing me the damage that was done to my heart from my father not being in my life. He was the obstacle that I was stumbling over, in which I needed to confront.

I had lived my life without ever really looking back and trying to understand the things I had gone through. I had encountered hurt, pain, suffering, and rejection as a child growing up, and for the life of me, I didn't understand it. After a while, I stopped trying to understand it because it all seemed futile.

At times, I would try to talk about my past with other people, but they couldn't give me what I was looking for. They would say "Oh, just keep it moving; you will be okay. Don't let your past hold you back. Let go of your past, and get on with your life."

Even though what they told me didn't help, I took it and ran with it because it was the only answer I had. Besides, I thought maybe I didn't need to understand my past. I honestly didn't think it would hurt me, so I left it alone.

As I got older, I realized that nobody advised me to deal with my past. All I heard was, "Run from your past, and don't deal with it." Now that I have a little wisdom, I understand that if you don't deal with your past, then it will deal with you. What you don't know *can* hurt you.

Those people who made those comments were running from their past and they had never dealt with it. They had never accepted or acknowledged what had been done to them. They had moved forward without ever dealing with their own issues. They may have moved on, but they were never healed, and the problems had not been solved.

How can you deal with something that you keep running from? Mike Murdock once said, "You will never be delivered from anything that you are unwilling to confront." The moment I heard that quote, my eyes were opened. I began to see myself in a whole different light.

I began to ask God to break me and show me myself. I knew He was the only one who could help me confront my past. I was tired of running from my past and acting like I had it all together. I was tired of pretending to other people like everything was going well in my life when I knew I was torn up inside.

GOD CANNOT HEAL WHAT YOU KEEP HIDDEN

Facing my past was a fight that I didn't think I was ready for. It was like a Band-Aid that had been left on a wound: once the Band-Aid is pulled off, you can feel the hurt and pain that was being covered, but once the wound is exposed, it can breathe and heal. I then realized that I couldn't keep the Band-Aid on my past anymore; I decided to ask God to remove it so I could breathe and heal.

God began showing me what I had been running from my whole life. He showed me how I had built my life on pain, hurt, rejection, bitterness, and insecurities. He showed me how I had used football to camouflage the pain because I was angry and upset that my father wasn't there for me when I was growing up. I guess I assumed that football would fix that problem, but it didn't solve any of my problems. It only allowed me to hide them by expressing my emotions through the game.

When the game was over, those problems and feelings were still there, alive and active. I thought that if I became successful in football, then my father would want me again. I thought that if I could prove myself to everybody else, then he would think I was worthy of being his son.

For the first time, I came to grips with the fact that I needed to be healed from the rejection of my father. My heart was empty and broken because I never knew my father. I was angry and bitter because my father was supposed to be there for me. He was supposed to teach me how to be a man and how to play football. I hid all of that pent-up aggression behind the game. I filled that emptiness in my heart with football in order to replace my father. When the game was gone, the emptiness was still there. I was still angry, bitter, lost, and confused because I had never dealt with it.

As a boy growing up, I didn't understand everything that was going on inside of me. I couldn't describe how I was feeling, so I did what boys naturally do: I found something I could love, and I attached myself to it. I loved football because it was all I had. It was an outlet that I could use to express how I felt about life.

I went back to when I was a child — when I thought that it was normal to not have a father. What I thought was normal was not really normal. I had adapted to the environment I was in because everybody else had done the same. I had adapted to an environment that said it was okay to grow up without a father, and that type of attitude and thinking kept me in bondage. I went back to when I heard my mother say my father didn't want me and that I was not his son. I did not realize that just hearing those words had been affecting me all this time.

At first, I didn't want to accept what God was showing me. It was too overwhelming. I didn't realize that I had been running from what I didn't want to face. People who knew me knew that I was likable, lovable, and easy to get along with. I was a standout athlete, got good grades in school, and tried to do the right thing. I never acknowledged that I had any problems because I was trying to present to people the image of a perfect person. I didn't want people to see me for who I really was.

I guess the Brandon Sweeney I portrayed to people was a fake because when I look back, I realize that I was actually hurting, and I was living a lie. No one could tell I was hurting because I was a great performer. Football made me a great performer — everybody loved me solely based on my athletic ability and what I could do for the coaches, fans, and players. I brought that mentality into my personal life. I was afraid that people would reject me if I were to simply be myself.

WHAT A BOY REALLY NEEDS IS HIS FATHER

It never occurred to me that the only thing I really wanted was my father to be in my life and to love on me. I wanted to be accepted, loved, affirmed, and confident in myself. I was looking for my father's voice to say, "Son, this is who you are. I am proud of you. You are great, etc." My mother gave me all the love, support, and encouragement she could. I was very grateful for that, but nothing can get a boy going more than a father who thinks the world of him.

A boy needs a father who loves him, encourages him, disciplines him, and supports him. A boy needs a father who can give him instructions on how to be a man, direction concerning where to go in life, vision to see where he is headed, and purpose to bring clarity to why he is here in this world. I longed in my heart as a boy to have a father to look up to. I wanted a father that could model myself after so that I could see myself in his reflection. I wanted a father that I could watch and study to see everything he did — to see how a man was supposed to live.

God revealed to me that I was trying to get my needs met through something that was never designed to meet those needs. He impressed upon my heart that I was empty because my father didn't fill that void. That emptiness in my life was reserved for a father, and anything else that tried to fill that void never lasted.

I thank God for Jesus Christ because He was able to fill those empty places with His love. God loved me so much that He sent His Son to die for me — to forgive me, deliver me, and heal me from everything I was going through. He was able to heal my heart by bringing me face to face with my past. I had to accept it and deal with the fact that my father wasn't a part of my life growing up. I began to forgive my father in my heart and not blame him anymore. I let go of all that bitterness and hatred that I had kept hidden in my heart because it was keeping me from moving forward, developing as a person, and enjoying God and life.

I had been blaming my dad for not raising me to be a man, and I had been treating God the same way. I wouldn't let Him get close to me; I kept Him at an arm's length because I thought He was going to hurt or reject me like my father did. Now, I was able to let my guard down when it came to building a relationship with God and other men. I realized that I needed godly men and mentors in my life to model true manhood, to offer their wisdom, and to lovingly confront me when I got out of line.

God revealed to me that He would do what my father didn't do because in His Word, He says He is a "father to the fatherless." When I allowed God to get close to me, He loved me and accepted me for who I was — the good, the bad, and the ugly.

After I allowed God to deal with me, my father showed up in my life. Most men would be upset and ready to fight, but not me. I invited him into my life so that I could spend what time I had left getting to know him. I wanted to know if I smiled like him, talked like him, thought like him. He apologized for everything he had done, and he wanted to explain; but like God does for us, I had already forgiven him before he came to me. I not only set myself free, but I also set him free from the guilt and regret he probably felt for not being in my life. I don't know why God worked it out the way He did, but I thank Him for it. Today, my father and I have a great relationship despite what took place in the past.

I am a witness that God can restore what was damaged or broken and redeem what was lost. My question to you is, "When are you going to deal with your past or the obstacle you keep stumbling over?" When are you going to forgive your father from your heart? When are you going to allow God to love on you without pushing Him away? The choice is yours, but as long as you wait to make a choice, you delay your development, healing, and deliverance.

Taken from Author Rick Johnson's book *Better Dads, Stronger Sons*, here are 7 ways to reconcile with your father. I wanted to include them here so that you can deal with your hurt and pain and begin to be healed.

RECONCILING WITH YOUR FATHER
1. *Pray for God to help you forgive and understand your father*
2. *Approach your father with an open heart*
3. *Find common ground—-don't condemn him with the past*
4. *Ask about his childhood and relationship with his father*

5. *Tell him you want to have a deeper relationship with him*
6. *Tell him that you love him, ask for his forgiveness if necessary*
7. *Honor him as God would command. If your father has died write him a letter from your heart. Share it with your mother if appropriate*

Everybody Has A Purpose

"More men fail through lack of purpose than lack of talent."
-Billy Sunday-

"Every young man we ignore becomes a candidate to cause us great harm in the future."
-Dr. Harold Davis-

The goal for athletes after playing sports should not be to adjust to life without sports but to a life that is purposeful and significant.
-Brandon Sweeney-

Education is good but knowing your purpose is better.
-Brandon Sweeney-

If ever an Athlete learns to see himself beyond playing sports, then he will have more success in life than the athlete who only has tunnel vision.
-Brandon Sweeney-

CHAPTER 16

Athletes Have a Purpose Beyond Playing Sports

After being reconciled with my father, I felt as if a load had been lifted off my shoulders. During that time, while God was taking me through that process of healing, I managed to stay in school — to continue to fight to finish. When 2008 came around, I was almost finished with school, and boy was I happy about it; after I realized that I couldn't play football anymore, everything else didn't seem to mean much to me. While I was in school, I went through the motions, dreading every moment of it, yet I still pressed on. I kept telling myself, "Get through the spring semester, and you will be done for good."

When I got to the end of the spring semester, I was ready to graduate, but I found out that I actually needed one more credit. My department explained to me that I could not graduate, and I could not walk across the stage. My heart dropped, and on the inside, I screamed, "NOOOOOOOOOOOOOOOOOO! How can this be?" I knew I had done everything right, so I went to the dean of the Construction department to try to get this straightened out, but there was nothing they could do. I left the office devastated, thinking, "I hung in there this whole time, and now they are telling me I cannot graduate. They don't know how hard it was for me to get this far and how much this process took out of me."

I wanted to give up and say "the heck with this" because I didn't think graduating from college was worth it anymore, but through the encouraging words of my mentors, friends, and church family, I decided to continue to fight. I then saw how important it was for me to get my degree. I started thinking about my family and the example I was setting for my brother and sisters. I started thinking about how I needed to finish what I had started, even though I didn't like school anymore; this wasn't about me. This was about breaking a generational cycle in my family. This was about being able to tell my children one day that I finished what I started — that I didn't quit because things got hard, but I hung in there and kept fighting. I understood then that I had to finish, close the chapter, and complete what I had started.

With that being said, I went to summer school to get my one credit, and I waited until December of the fall semester to walk across that stage. Boy, what a feeling that was. I was so proud of myself because I could have given up and made excuses for why I didn't finish my degree, but instead, I chose to finish. At this point, you would have thought that life was going to be sweet. Not so!

WHEN YOU DON'T UNDERSTAND THE PURPOSE OF EDUCATION, YOU WILL ABUSE IT.

After I graduated, I came home, sat down, and started thinking about my life. After thinking for some time, I became frustrated. I had received a degree that should have only taken me four years to complete but ended up taking me six years. However, it wasn't the amount of time it took me to get my degree that frustrated me — it was the fact that I hated the degree I had chosen. There was nothing in me that wanted to work in the field of construction, despite the fact that I could work with my hands pretty well. I had never thought of using my major after college because my dream was to play in the NFL. I wondered, "How did this happen?"

It was then that I started to realize that as an athlete I have been fooling myself and others. All I ever heard was, "Get your education, make sure you keep your grades up, and stay eligible for the season." Well, I got an education, I got the good grades, and I finished college, but I found myself still unfulfilled and unsatisfied. I asked myself, "Is this what I have been working for all these years?" Then I asked, "Have I done all of this just so I could stay eligible for sports and get a job?" All of these thoughts ran through my mind while I was trying to figure out what went wrong.

Then it hit me. The answer came to me as clear as day concerning why I was unfulfilled and unsatisfied. It was because I was just going through the motions during school. I was programmed by coaches and teachers to think that if I maintained my grades and stayed out of trouble, I would be okay. So what do you think I did? I met the requirements of middle school, high school, and college. I maintained a good grade point average, stayed out of trouble, and chose a major. According to NCAA rules, I couldn't go into my junior year without deciding on a major, so of course, with my heart set on going pro, I chose something that was easy and that wouldn't interfere with me playing football.

Now, to be clear, there is no room to point the finger at anybody else; I take responsibility for my actions and the decisions I made. I am simply stating the facts when I say that most athletes choose their majors without ever thinking about whether they will use their degrees once they can no longer play sports. This is why we have seen a lot of athletes frustrated, disappointed, and hurt; they got their degrees, but when they could no longer play the sports they loved, their degrees didn't matter. In fact, some athletes only finished getting their degrees to make their parents or families proud. Other athletes simply quit going to school when they realized their dreams were not coming to pass. All I can say is, "What a tragedy."

Here is what's wrong with this kind of thinking. Athletes aren't set up to discover what they are created to do beyond sports. They don't know what else they are good at other than playing sports. They don't even know what other talents they possess besides running fast, throwing, kicking, shooting, or hitting a ball. But then, why would they when all they do is perfect their game? When they finally discover their God-given purpose, education will become more meaningful. They will then begin to center their lives around their overall purpose and not just playing sports. Even if their dreams of playing professionally come true, they will still know that they are more than athletes, and they will have a bigger picture of their lives. Every athlete should start thinking outside the box because if they do not, then they will be trapped and could be considered labeled as "Small-Minded." Athletes, you have a purpose that has yet to be discovered.

I'M MORE THAN JUST AN ATHLETE

After I discovered this revelation, I knew I had to do something about it. I couldn't sit there watching my life pass me by. I saw too many athletes give up on life because they couldn't make the transition from sports to life successfully. Even though I knew my career playing football was over, I had remembered what God told me. He said, "The only reason you are still hanging onto football is because you don't believe that I have something better for you." At this point in my walk with God, I was more confident in Him and trusted that He would help me through this like He did with everything else. At the same time, I wanted to find out what God meant by "better" and this time I was determined to find out and get an answer.

I did what I normally did; I started seeking God to find out what He had in store for me. After a few weeks of praying, I started to become weary because nothing was coming to me. I had no answers and no sign of what God meant by "better". Then one day, He gave me an idea while I was with my mentor, Alan Hooker. We were sharing ideas about a lot of different things; I liked being around Hook because he was so inspiring and motivating that I couldn't help but be encouraged by the time I left his presence. We had gotten on the subject of sports because at that time, I was coaching football at a high school while trying to figure out what I was going to do with my life. Hook started talking about athletes and coaching, and while I was listening, a statement came across my mind. I don't know if this was God or me, but the statement was, **"You are more than just an athlete."** When I heard that statement, my whole perception of myself was changed. I went home that night inspired, and I knew I was on to something.

WHEN THE RIGHT QUESTIONS ARE ASKED, THEN THE ANSWERS WILL APPEAR.

When I arrived at home, all I could do was think about that statement. As I sat there, questions begin to flood my mind and I started writing them down as fast as I could. I knew that these questions were clues that would help me discover what God was calling me to do. I then began asking God, myself, friends, and families these questions to see what they had thought about me.

If you want to start discovering your God-given purpose, then write these questions down, and begin to answer them for yourself. Pray and ask God to reveal things to you about yourself that you didn't know. Ask family, friends, and coaches to assist you. Be patient with yourself because the answers may not come right away. Also, test your answers to see if they are true, and if they are not, then go back and narrow things down or scratch them. Remember, this is a journey, a discovery, so get excited because God is about to blow your mind.

13 QUESTIONS/CLUES TO HELP YOU START THE PROCESS OF DISCOVERING YOUR GOD-GIVEN PURPOSE AND IDENTITY:

*Below are my answers to these questions to give you an idea of how I answered them.

#1: **Who Am I?**
- I am a Child of God
- Motivator

- Encourager
- Coach

#2: Why Am I Here?
- To glorify God in all I do;
- To help put men back in their proper positions to lead their wives and families;
- To help people walk in freedom and purpose.

#3: What other spiritual and natural gifts do I possess?
- The gift of helping other people,
- Exhorting,
- Encouraging,
- Leadership,
- Pastoring,
- Prophesying
- Speaking.

#4: What skills have I learned from playing football?
The skills I have acquired are :
- Communication,
- Listening,
- Time management,
- Being a team player,
- Problem solving,
- Decision making,
- Planning,

- Organizing,
- Empathizing,
- Leading,
- Delegating.

#5: What else am I passionate about other than sports?
- I am passionate about following Jesus Christ,
- I am passionate about helping athletes become better men, and helping them discover their true identities and purposes in life beyond sports.
- I am passionate about helping the fatherless deal with their problems regarding their father.
- I am passionate about families and seeing fathers back in the home.
- I am passionate about mentoring young men.
- I am passionate about helping people become everything that God wants them to be.

#6: What do I hate so much that I want to change?
- I hate seeing boys grow up without fathers,
- Athletes and people waste their potential
- People give up on their dreams or life.
- Single moms raising kids all by themselves,
- Men who abandon their children
- Those who exploit the fatherless for their own profit. In particular in sports.

#7: What do I love doing — what comes naturally to me?
- I love listening to and helping people solve their problems
- I naturally bring out the best in people
- I naturally encourage people.
- I love coaching athletes and people to become better.
- I naturally lead or take charge when placed in a group
- I love being around entrepreneurs, dreamers, coaches, sports teams, and leaders

#8: What group of people do I love being around or would like to help?
- I like to help athletes and the fatherless young men because they unlock my compassion.

#9: What do people always come to me for?
- People come to me for advice, encouragement, motivation, and inspiration.

#10: In what Domain (Field) do I fit in? Domain (field) means an area where your gifts are better suited.
- Education Field
- Coaching Field
- Counseling field
- Public speaking field

#11: What type of education would I need to fulfill to purse my passion?

- Master's Degree in Sports and Exercise Psychology
- Read great books in the fields that I am interested in

#12: What words do my family members, coaches, teachers, friends, and mentors use to describe me? What do they see in me that I don't see in myself?
- Determined
- Destined for greatness
- Hard worker
- Resilient,
- Quick learner,
- Wise beyond my years
- Teachable
- Always learning,
- Passionate
- Compassionate
- Change agent
- A go-getter,
- Natural born leader,
- People person,
- Great listener,
- Loyal,
- Trustworthy,
- Responsible.

#13: How do you best learn?
- Observing

- Practicing
- Visualizing

I am able to answer these questions now, but when I first tried to answer them, I didn't have a clue. I would write down what I thought I knew, but after God began to show me over time the person I was becoming, the answers became clearer. I went through a lot of trial and error because I would test what I wrote down, and if it didn't line up, I would scratch it. For example, I started working in a group home because I knew I wanted to work with young men. While there, I found out a lot about myself that I didn't realize before. I found out that I didn't like the group home setting or dealing with kids with certain conditions, so I went back to the drawing board and found out that I loved mentoring young men on my own time. It allowed me to assist them more, without all the limitations.

Another example: I loved counseling people, so I thought, "Why not continue to work with youth in the mental health field?" After being in the field for seven years, I was burned out, and the little zeal that I had faded away. I went back to the drawing board to figure out what group of people I wanted to work with and discovered that it was young men who were athletes. When I narrowed everything down, it all made sense. Every time I got around athletes, something in me would come alive that I couldn't explain. Anytime I had a chance to speak to them or mentor them, I would get excited and give them everything I had because I was that passionate about what I was doing.

So don't get the impression that everything happened all at once after I first answered those questions because it didn't. I had to take those pieces to the puzzle and put them together, and for a long time, I didn't know how everything would fit. Now, I am closer than I was five years ago. Not only that, but I have decided to go back to school to get my master's in Sports and Exercise Psychology, and I am more focused and prepared for school now than I was when I first started. I know now why I am going to get my master's: I have used these clues and questions to bring me close to understanding my purpose, and this degree will help me fulfill it. I am not there yet but I am on the right track.

YOU CHOOSE: YOUR PLAN OR GOD'S PLAN?

Things finally started making sense to me. For the first time in my life, my eyes were opened, and I could see clearly. It was like my life was a big book that was opened before me and God was showing me, "ME." I saw how God's plan for my life was so much greater than what I had planned for myself. He was showing me the bigger picture by expanding the vision I had of myself.

> **Key Bible Verses to Read:**
> Jeremiah 29:11, Psalms 37:23, Psalms 139,
> Proverbs 16:9, Proverbs 19:21, and Proverbs 20:24.

I felt so much joy on the inside of me because it seemed like I was discovering treasure in me that I never knew existed. I became encouraged again and excited about life because what had seemed like the end of me was only the beginning. That's when I learned the principle that *you should never get stuck on one chapter when you haven't finished reading the rest of the book; keep reading because it gets better.*

Life was looking better for me because I was walking on the right path. That one statement, "You are more than just an athlete," changed my life. I almost wasted the untapped potential that was lying dormant in me because I only saw myself as an athlete. I had no idea what God had put on the inside of me. I had no idea I would be writing this book, going to get a master's degree, starting a business, and going around speaking. I had my life mapped out. I had tunnel vision and couldn't break out of it. He had so much planned for me, but I almost missed out on it because I had my own plan and I thought it was better than God's. I wanted to do my own thing because I couldn't see how God's plan would work, but now I understand that if God ever has to interrupt my dreams, goals, or plans, it only means that they weren't big enough because they didn't include Him.

Your dream of going pro may not have worked out like you planned, but rest assured that God has a plan for your life. It is bigger and better and beyond your wildest imagination, but you have to let go; you must let go to receive what God has for you. I can say with a sincere heart that I don't miss playing football, not one bit, because I have a new vision, mission, and purpose that I am chasing. So, it's your choice: you can choose your plan or God's plan.

Brandon speaking at an event to promote his latest book.

CHAPTER 17

A Word to Parents and Coaches: What a Difference You Make!

I want to end this book by first thanking all sports parents and coaches for doing what you do, day in and day out. Parents, you don't get the recognition you deserve for raising a young woman or young man as an athlete. It is not easy, but you always seem to make time for your children because you want the best for them. You make sports worthwhile because you give your children permission to play, and you entrust coaches with the responsibility to teach and train your children to become great athletes. For that, I want to say thank you. Thank you for believing in your child, for wanting the best for them, and for going above and beyond. Parents, you are the real MVPs.

I want to thank and congratulate all the coaches who have taken time to not only build great athletes but great men and women. If no one has ever praised you or thanked you for what you do, day in and day out, then I certainly will because that job is not easy. You deserve to be recognized and applauded because not many have the guts to do what you do.

You don't get the recognition you deserve for helping young men become great fathers, husbands, friends, and productive members of society, or for helping young women become great mothers, wives, friends, and productive members of society. You know more than anyone that the reward that comes from pouring into their lives is worth more than anything. Because of your influence, love, guidance, advice, and support, they are better people now than they were before they came to you. I pray that every coach will catch this idea and run with it. Winning is important, but nothing is as important as helping a boy become a man or a girl become a woman — helping them find their purpose in life and training them to become leaders in all aspects of life.

My story and the stories of other athletes burn deep within me, and I cannot be silent about the concerns and issues I have with sports and what is happening to athletes all over this world. I believe that some people have caught the revelation about building not just great athletes, but great men and women, as well. However, a large number of coaches and parents have diverted themselves from the true purpose of sports. I want to address that issue in this chapter.

COACHES, WHAT YOU SAY AND DO LEAVES AN IMPRINT ON YOUR ATHLETES

I have seen coaches take advantage of fatherless men (knowing they have nobody else to look up to) by using their athletic ability to build their programs and to help them win games. When playing time was up, however, the coaches didn't have anything to do with them. I have seen so many coaches become consumed with winning a game rather than winning a life, with building a program rather than building men.

I have seen so many guys sacrifice their lives for coaches by putting in time, hard work, and loyalty, but they get nothing in return. Some coaches provide false information on how to become a man. They demonstrate, not just through words but by their actions, what a "real man" should look like, but it is far from the truth.

I have seen coaches say one thing but do another, yet they expect players to have integrity. I have seen coaches become so consumed with the team that they neglect individual players. Some coaches are not even concerned with the personal lives of players unless they interfere with sports. I have seen coaches break and tear men and women apart with their words, thinking that verbal abuse was the key to motivating them to work harder. I have seen coaches say that it is all about the team, but in reality, it's all about them.

I only had a few coaches in all of my years of playing football that tried to make me a better man as well as a great athlete. They talked to me about how to treat women, about giving my life to Jesus Christ, learning to trust God, waiting until marriage to have sex, leading as a man in life (not just in football), saving money, being responsible, how to treat my parents, how to treat people in general, and how to act outside of sports.

They provided me with information to think about, information I didn't have before, and they gave me a choice to make. They got my attention, not just by what they were telling me, but by the fact that they were living it...and that made a huge difference!

Looking back on my life, I probably would have chosen to follow their advice and the information they gave me if it had been reinforced by the other coaches I came across. I only had a few coaches who were brave and bold enough to tell me the truth, but their information and advice went in one ear and out the other. Why? I had other coaches who were telling me and showing me something very different.

Some coaches would tell me the right things to do, but they lived the complete opposite of what they said. Some would tell me to thank God and live for God, but then they would curse me out later on, thinking that it would get my attention. I guess they thought I was used to it because I grew up in the projects.

I thank God for people like Tony Dungy, who decided not to use foul language while he was coaching, and for all those great coaches whom the media does not mention.

I have heard coaches say it's okay to have sex with as many girls as you want: "I know you are young, but just be careful, and wear a condom." Yet, when a player would catch an STD that he couldn't get rid of, or when a player would get a girl pregnant, then that coach didn't want to help or support them. He would say things like, "Be a man, and handle your responsibility. Get a blood test to see if the baby is yours because women tend to trap athletes who are going pro."

These coaches say things like, "It's okay to drink and smoke, but make sure you are clear when drug screening comes up so that you're ready for the big game. After all, we need you."

Some coaches say, "I don't care about your grades, as long as you're eligible for the season." Then they tell them to get an education and become a student athlete.

How can athletes become better people when their coaches are not living their best? How can they walk in integrity when the only definition or reference point they have for integrity is their coach? How can they succeed in life when their coaches are only concerned about winning?

> "Whatever affects one directly, affects all indirectly. I can never be what I ought to be until you are what you ought to be. This is the interrelated structure of reality." -**Martin Luther King, Jr.**

One thing coaches have to understand is that they might be the only man in a boy's life who can model what a man should look and act like. They might be the only woman who can demonstrate how a real woman should live. It is said that a team naturally takes on the mindset of its leader. If that is the case, misguided coaches produce a lot of misguided players.

Whatever standard a coach lives by — good or bad — some of the players will follow. If you as a coach don't have yourself together, then for the most part, they won't have themselves together. If all you teach is "win even if you have to cheat" or that it's okay for a teacher to pull strings for a failing athlete or that an athlete is not held accountable, then that is all they will ever know.

You can't just say good things and expect good results. If you are displaying these negative traits, then your words mean nothing. Be a man before you show them how to be men; lead before you show them how to lead; love before you show them how to love, and your players will follow.

Sports is a business, especially on the collegiate and pro levels, but what will it cost for you to better yourself so that your players can better themselves? What will it take for you to sow positive seeds into another person's life?

It might cost you your job or the program that you are building with wrong motives. It might cost you time, effort, energy, or a pay cut. You just have to decide if it is worth it!

In the book *Season of Life* by Jeffrey Marx, Joe Ehrmann, who is considered a Coach for America said that the way his team measures greatness is by the impact they have on other people's lives. The book also profiled the head coach of Gilman High School, who was asked a question by one of the parents. The parent asked how things were looking for the season and how successful the team would be that year. The head coach, Biff, said he had no idea and would not know until 20 years later. The lady said, "Huh?" Biff went on to explain that he wouldn't know how successful they had been until the players came back to visit in 20 years. Then he would be able to see what kind of fathers and husbands they had become and what they were doing in the community.

Joe Ehrmann also stated that their goal was to build men for others through relationships. How powerful is that! They were not building men for their team, for the men themselves, or for the coaches but for their friends, family, and community as a whole.

The main agenda for these coaches was to demonstrate love to their players daily, regardless of whether they performed well or poorly. The team's agenda was to love one another. There is not enough of that going around in the football arena.

Coaches, if you really care about a player and his/her future outside of sports, then you won't have to worry about winning games or championships because players will play for a coach cares of them and has their best interest at heart.

I had no problem playing for my high school coach, Robert Proctor, because he cared for me. I didn't want to disappoint him; I wanted to give him my best because he gave me his best.

If you touch the hearts of men and women, everything else will fall in line; but how many are willing to step outside of their comfort zones to do that? What a difference that would have made in my life at a young age! I don't blame anybody for the way I ended up because it all worked together for my good in the end, but I would have been further along had I had coaches who cared.

PARENTS, YOUR CHILD'S LIFE SHOULD NOT BE ALL ABOUT SPORTS

I have seen parents pressure their children to play sports for several reasons: to gain a college scholarship, to learn how to be tough, or to go pro so that they could reap the rewards. I have seen parents pour so much time and money into their child's future with sports that their child never has a balanced life. Sports is the focal point of the child's life.

I have seen parents try to send their kids to a winning school because they want them to be noticed by professional recruiters or scouts. I have seen parents put sports over both formal and informal education. Some kids don't even have a chance to decide what they want to be because their parents have already decided for them. I have seen parents use their own kid's athletic ability to make money so they would be taken care of in the future.

Some parents never show their kids that there is more to life than sports or that there is more than one way to go to college and succeed in life. Some parents set their children up for failure when they allow their child to put all their eggs (e.g. hopes and dreams) into one basket (Sports).

I am not saying that you should not support your child's dream or that you should neglect his dream. If you think he will be heartbroken by not participating, just encourage him to bring balance to his life. Give your children options, provide the right information (like some of my coaches did for me), and reinforce it. Ultimately, they will have to choose which road to take. When you give them only one option, you rob them of reaching their full potential and finding their purpose.

WE CAN USE SPORTS TO BUILD STRONG MEN AND WOMEN.

I need coaches who won't compromise, who have a desire to build great athletes and great men and women. I need coaches who are willing to pour into the life of an athlete who has no father or mentor.

I need parents who will not allow their child to be coached by someone who is not willing to help him/her become a better man or woman, no matter how good the coach is or how many championships he has won. I need parents who will help coaches teach and train their children the right way by giving them balanced lives.

I need players who will admit they need help — that they need fatherly advice and wisdom. I need them to want more than just sports for their lives. I need players who are willing to put away childish things and become men and women.

I hope that players, coaches, and parents will not just settle for a great athlete but that they will desire a great man or woman, great husband or wife, great leader, great brother or sister, great friend, and great father or mother.

I'm looking for those who desire to break the cycle of men growing up without fathers, of men who don't know who they are and why they are here.

I believe that if men ever get back into the position where they belong, as the head of the family, then women, children, and whole families will fall in line. We can use Sports to do that. We can use it to rebuild broken men, attack this issue of fatherlessness, and impact the family system. But all of us have to step up and desire the same thing.

I LEAVE YOU WITH THIS:

If we are not helping raise up our young men and women, then why are we involved in this sports? If we are not willing to let God use us to change a young person's life, then why are we involved?

We will all give an account before God one day, and I believe He will ask the coach, "What did you do with the players I sent to you? The ones that needed to know what a man or woman looked like, to prepare them for life — how did you treat them?"

To the player: "What did you do with and how did you treat the coaches and parents that I put in your life to help you become a man or woman?"

To the parent: "What did you do with the children I gave you? How did you prepare them for their futures? What did you do with and how did you treat the coaches I sent to you to help you change your children's lives?"

What will your answer be? What will you tell God?

-Appendix-
Real-Life Athletes' Stories About Their Love for Sports and Their Transition

I caught up with some athletes that I'd either played football with or against growing up and some other friends whom I'd met throughout my career in sports. I wanted to share their stories to show other athletes that they are not alone. To all the athletes out there, other people have been where you are and yet have found purpose beyond playing sports. There is hope for all of the hopeless ex-athletes whose dreams have been crushed, and there is wisdom for those still playing to start preparing now instead of later. I hope that this helps you as you start your journey of discovering both your identity and your purpose beyond sports.

KAMERON ALEXANDER

At an early age, like most athletes, Kameron fell in love with football. He was just as passionate about the game as the next man. He worked hard and dedicated himself to becoming a standout athlete. However, during his senior year in college, he played in a game against Ferris State and broke his thumb. That was a sad and depressing day because he knew things wouldn't be the same. Kameron felt like he'd lost everything. He had no hopes for a future, and he certainly didn't have a plan in place.

Kameron shut himself inside his apartment for about two weeks and began living in denial about the reality that he could no longer play football. He began missing class because it seemed like nothing else mattered to him. Then one day, Kameron discovered that there was more to life than just football. That day, Kameron decided to become more than an athlete and started discovering other talents God had given him. He found out that he had acquired skills that he could use in his career. Now, Kameron is working at a bank in Akron, Ohio and putting his skills and talents to use in a field he loves. Kameron has also been helping other athletes by encouraging them to see life beyond sports.

Kameron is happy with the accomplishments he has achieved through football because they have made him a better man.

MARQUES RUFFIN

Marques Ruffin was a standout athlete at North Carolina A&T State University. For as long as Marques could remember, all he knew was football. He had no idea what he liked to do outside of football. He felt that there was nothing else in life that was fulfilling other than going to the NFL and making a lot of money.

Later on, a question was posed to Marques about what life after football was like. He replied by saying, "Well honestly, football is not over for me because I am still pursuing my dream." Marques said that he was under the illusion that the best place for him after college was in the NFL.

As promising career opportunities in the work force knocked at his door, he ignored them so that he could pursue a dream that really had no interest in pursuing him. At the end of his football career, he was lost. When it came to finding a career, he had no clue which direction to take, mainly because there was nothing else he was passionate about. Marques discovered that when his career in football ended, he was not ready for life in the work force.

In his own honest assessment, his transition was very trying. Outside of football, he had no real purpose that was bigger than himself and his plans. He was only thinking of what was most beneficial for himself and not what he could do for the betterment of something or someone other than himself. That mentality guided his career pursuits; every career interest was based on how much money he could make rather than how much he could make an impact. He wished he would have learned somewhere throughout his career in sports that he should live for more than himself and all of his personal accomplishments.

There were times when he would beat himself up, throw a pity party, or play the blame game because his mother never let him get a job while growing up. He felt that working at a younger age would have given him some idea that work was synonymous with the real world and that life was not always about a game. At times, he felt like he should have pushed himself to get good grades rather than settling for being average. He kicked himself for forgetting that strength in the area of academics relates to success in the work force.

Overall, football has truly been for Marques both a gift and a curse, allowing him to attain a debt-free college degree in four years but also allowing him to live in a dream world where he had no sense of what the real world was like when the game was over. He is truly thankful for the game, but he sometimes wishes football would have taught him more practical values and life lessons.

Today, Marques has discovered a new passion: coaching and teaching high school athletes, as well as ministering to teenagers in his local church. Marques feels like his gift is to encourage, and he uses that gift to help teenagers maximize their opportunities in life.

JIMMY LAMOUR

The day that sports ended for Jimmy was a true "wake-up" call. He first realized that he might not play the game of football again when his senior year of college football was ending. He knew that going pro was a "long shot" with him playing at a Division 3 college program. However, God blessed him to have a great career there, and his head coach received several phone calls from NFL teams that were interested in him. The Green Bay Packers, New Orleans Saints, Cleveland Browns, and Jacksonville Jaguars were all showing interest, but they all said that he needed to play against higher competition and should explore the arena football league. He was devastated; he played in some arena football leagues, but he knew that his opportunity was fading away. Furthermore, he was married now and had two children. He knew that his responsibilities should shift, but he was still holding onto the dream inwardly. In fact, he wanted a job that would not interfere with his training schedule, even though he could have had better opportunities to provide for his family. Life became mundane, and he felt like all his hopes and dreams were destroyed. The "thing" he put all his hope and trust in to provide for his family was gone.

He questioned God and went into a deep depression. He was angry with his wife and children because he felt they were a hindrance to his pursuit of the game he loved. It led to a decline in his marriage, which was on the brink of divorce, and he realized at that point that he never planned for life after football. He thought if he had explored other options, it would have shown that he did not believe that God could help him go pro. Only with much prayer, rededication to God, his wife's urging, and coaching his son's football team did he realize that God was calling him to train young men athletically and mentally. Lamour Training Systems was born in 2005, and it continues to this day.

To find out more about Jimmy Lamour, visit his website: www.ltscombinecamps.com

AUSTIN CLOPTIN

When sports ended for Austin, he was in the fourth game of his senior year in college. He remembers it like it was yesterday. It was the second play of the game when he was tackled. He thought he had a stinger in his left shoulder. He came to find out that his vertebra was smashed, and the main nerve that controlled his left arm was damaged, as well. He lost all the muscle in his left arm, and it was paralyzed for almost a week. The neurologist told him that he was done playing forever. When he heard the news, he didn't know what to say or do because playing sports was all he had ever known. He told the doctor he would play again, and he played in the last three games of his 10-1 senior season.

After college, he had an opportunity to play professional football; however, he felt like something was telling him to use his abilities to help others, and that's what he did. He graduated with a Sports Management degree and knew he wanted to work in sports — something that he had loved so much growing up — so he became a high school football coach at his alma mater, Garfield High School in Akron, OH.

After networking with some people and working in some football camps, he knew exactly what he needed to do in his hometown: help the youth. He teamed up with his business partner, Steve Reynolds, and created Most Known Unknown Athletics (MKU Athletics). At first, they wanted to do anything and everything to help their youth excel in sports. They implemented camps and trainings, and they created highlight films for their youth. Since then, they have turned this passion into a legitimate business. They have helped their youth get into college, understand "hard work", identify their weaknesses, and turn those weaknesses into strengths. Their business has brought the attention of ESPN scouts to some of their workouts to see their athletes compete against each other during the off-season.

They are blessed to be in a position to help so many young athletes in the Akron, OH area. They look forward to continuing to build their youth and prepare them for life.

Austin is the Vice President and the COO of MKU Athletics. To find out more about what he does, visit their website at www.mkuathletics.com. Their slogan: #WeWorkin #BecomeKnown

DERRICK EMANUEL

There is a thin line between life and football! Just like a lot of athletes all over the world, Derrick was captivated by football at an early age. For him, life after football was a little tough because he had played the game since he was nine years old. He could never really see himself without football because it was a way of life. He knew that every season he would suit up, awaiting the smell of the locker room, shoulder pads, and grass. He was not fully prepared for life afterwards because he had no plan B or C written out. If he did have a plan it boggled up in his head. He became a teacher and coach right after college. He realized that God graced him to see the world in a different light, despite the fact that he had been so blinded by the poor choices he'd made based on how he viewed football.

The way he viewed football led him to believe that without out, he had no real identity, confidence, or purpose. His whole world was really based on loving a game that never committed to him, but he put all his feelings and emotions into it nonetheless. This eventually affected the way he communicated in relationships, education, and family. He thought all these people and things owed him something, and he felt like he could go at his own pace without making the appropriate sacrifices for them.

After football ended, he learned that he had a lot to offer through his other talents, and he discovered transferable skills that would help him fuel his purpose for life and for Jesus Christ. Positive friends, mentors, and family members showed him that he could be accountable, committed, dependable, and focused on his priorities in life. He has been away from playing the game since 2008 but he knows that one of his gifts is helping young men reach their full potential through his words of encouragement and love.

TIM SHROPSHIRE

Timothy Shropshire was pursuing his dream of playing football on the collegiate and professional levels. He was an athlete who did just enough to get by academically, and when asked what he wanted to major in, he said, "...something pertaining to sports." Why? Because that was what he truly cared about in life. While at North Carolina A&T State University, he lost his scholarship and was removed from the team for one year due to insignificant academic progress. This was his reality check; he began to gain more of an appreciation for education. He realized that he was getting ready to graduate with a major in sports science that knew nothing about. He inquired about how he could learn more about his field, and most of all, how he could pull up his significantly low GPA. He ultimately did. He graduated with a 2.6 GPA, became the Athletic Chaplain of his school, and became an NCAA Leadership Candidate.

God entered into his life at just the right time, or should I say God opened his eyes, because technically, God had been there from the start. God truly showed him His glory and showed him that he was much more than just a football player. He was God's son with a purpose to fulfill: Gods Purpose During that difficult year, Tim read a book written by the late great Bishop Otis Lockett Sr., *Understanding Your Divine Calling*. After reading the book, he realized that not only did he love to play football, but he also loved making people laugh. His love for laughter caused him to embrace the art of comedy. He was always known as the class clown or the football team comic, but never did he foresee himself performing on stage. In 2008, he did just that. Not only did he take the stage, but he also started his own management company and co-managed an entertainment company.

Comedy has permitted him to participate in events from the Virgin Islands to the Bayou of Louisiana. His ultimate goal is to conduct a world tour (including a tour throughout the U.S.), transforming his gift into a career opportunity. In addition to that, his mission is always to introduce people to Christ through comedy. To ensure his success, he regularly meets with a team of mentors who challenge and perfect his talent. He leans close to God for both provision to develop his comedic material and guidance on important life choices. Along with comedy, he wants to help athletes who are like he was — struggling with identity outside of football — and most of all, those who lack life skills. He found that even though he chose to find his purpose in life, he still struggled in a professional work environment because he lacked experience and professional skills. He had to work twice as hard as his coworkers but in the end, it paid off for him.

To find out more about Tim, visit his website: www.timshropcomedy.com

QUANTE SPEIGHT

Quante' didn't begin playing the game of football until he was in the 7th grade. He was first introduced to the game of baseball because that was the only sport his town provided on an official recreational platform. The cliché in his hometown was, "Either you do the negative things or you chose the positive ones to get by." Quante' decided to go with the positive route after seeing many of his close friends and family members opt for the life of crime.

Sports were everything to Quante'. Athletics truly came easy to him: diving to catch baseballs, attacking the basket to make explosive layups, running faster than everyone else, and imitating professional players on the football field, such as Bo Jackson, Barry Sanders, and Deion Sanders. When he started playing scholastic sports in 7th grade, he played baseball, basketball, football, and ran track; he never stopped playing all four sports until his senior year of high school when he had to leave baseball behind because he had fallen in love with football.

Throughout his childhood, from elementary through middle school, he was always considered a very intelligent student; he was labeled "Academically Gifted" and was always on the honor roll. Once he got to high school, he was placed in the honors classes. The work wasn't very difficult for him, but for some reason, he only did enough to get by and never felt the need to study. He believed he was only there to play sports, and it showed when he graduated with a 2.41 GPA and scored just barely high enough on the SAT (which he only took once) to get into college but not high enough to sign a letter of intent for football. He was not permitted to play football his first year of school.

He was overlooked by a lot of major universities that were trying to recruit him due failing grades. He ended up finding a school that had some interest in him, and he went on to play at North Carolina Agricultural & Technical State University for three seasons. While there, he dealt with some injuries yet still managed to have some success. He received numerous awards for his performance at NC A&T.

After the football season Quante' experienced some tough times at NC A&T. He went from playing college football on Saturdays to deciding to give it all up on the Monday after the 3rd game of his senior season. He didn't know what he wanted to do with his life or what was next for him, but through his newfound belief in the Lord and with the assistance of his beautiful wife, he found hope.

It wasn't until he stopped to reflect on his life and saw that he was more than an athlete that he began taking his education seriously. He wanted to build a future that he wouldn't have to give up when his legs and body began to age or slow down. Quante' decided to step outside the box of "just being an athlete" and broke the mold to become more. Quante' feels that he has learned a lot of life lessons from football that he will apply in his life and cherish forever. Quante' finished his degree at North Carolina A&T State University and went on to get his Master's in Health & Physical Education. Quante' now teaches and coaches football and track at the high school level in Greensboro, NC. Quante' is enjoying both his family and a career that he is passionate about.

References

Malone, H. (1999). Shadow Boxing: The Dynamic 2-5-14 Strategy to Defeat the Darkness Within. Vision Life Publishing, Lewisville, TX

Marx, J. (2003). Season of Life: A Football Star, a Boy, a Journey to Manhood. Simon & Schuste Publishing. New York, NY

Stankovich, C., Meeker, D., & Kays, T (2000). Positives Transitions for student athletes: Life Skills for Transitions in Sport, College, and Career. Holcomb Hathaway Publishing, Scottsdale, AZ